IMMORTAL

How I Learned There IS Life After Death

Diana Hewson

BALBOA
PRESS
A DIVISION OF HAY HOUSE

Balboa Press books may be ordered through booksellers or by contacting:
Balboa Press
A Division of Hay House
1663 Liberty Drive
Bloomington, IN 47403
www.balboapress.com
1-(877) 407-4847

Because of the dynamic nature of the Internet, any Web addresses or links contained in this book may have changed since publication and may no longer be valid. The views expressed in this work are solely those of the author and do not necessarily reflect the views of the publisher, and the publisher hereby disclaims any responsibility for them.

The author of this book does not dispense medical advice or prescribe the use of any technique as a form of treatment for physical, emotional, or medical problems without the advice of a physician, either directly or indirectly. The intent of the author is only to offer information of a general nature to help you in your quest for emotional and spiritual well-being. In the event you use any of the information in this book for yourself, which is your constitutional right, the author and the publisher assume no responsibility for your actions.

Any people depicted in stock imagery provided by Thinkstock are models, and such images are being used for illustrative purposes only. Certain stock imagery © Thinkstock.

ISBN: 978-1-4525-3204-2 (sc)
ISBN: 978-1-4525-3205-9 (e)

Printed in the United States of America

Balboa Press rev. date: 01/31/2011

For Ed

The center of my universe

I know we will be together for eternity.

Contents

PREFACE

My husband, Ed, passed away suddenly of a heart attack in May of 2003. We were extremely close and had somewhat isolated ourselves from friends since we mainly enjoyed just being together. We had no children and no close relatives. Initially, I had a hard time comprehending what had happened. It all seemed surreal. But I knew that it was up to me to proceed with life. In the past, we had had many conversations about life without children or anyone to depend on. I knew I had to be strong, but the reality and finality of losing my husband and best buddy made it hard to continue. I would never be able to see or talk with him again. We had talked with each other every day even when we were both travelling on business.

I have done my share of crying and feeling like I could not go on. But I never went on drugs and I only went to a bereavement group for a couple of months during the next winter's holiday season. Also unlike many people in grief, I never became mad or upset with my husband. I loved him too much.

Ed and I had been married for thirty-four years. Neither of us was religious and neither of us believed in life after death. Ed was particularly emphatic about his beliefs and never even wanted a funeral or anyone "praying over" him when he died. When he did die, I had several friends tell me that Ed would be communicating since we were so close. I told them I appreciated the thoughts and wished they were right, but I did not believe they were. Then unexplainable things began to happen. And about four months after his passing, Ed managed to make me a believer. With Ed's help and continued communications, I began to be able to proceed in handling life by myself. I began a campaign to read and learn as much as I could about life after death. I wanted to understand what Ed had been through and what he was experiencing.

This is my amazing story of how I learned that when someone close dies, it is not an end to the relationship. The relationship merely changes form. Of course, I would rather have Ed here in the flesh, but I know now that he is still with me, helping me through life. He has communicated this in many different ways so that now I *know* it is true. I *know* there is life after death.

I want to thank all the people who shared their experiences with me to help promote my understanding. Many names have been changed to protect their privacy. I have not made up any of these stories, but have represented them as they were related to me. I believe them all to be true.

I especially want to thank my friend and very gifted medium, Pat Gagliardo, who gave me permission to use her full name. Without her help, guidance and accurate messages, I would not have been able to move on with life as well as I have. I felt like I was having conversations with Ed. I needed these conversations to confirm that Ed was alive and in a better place.

CHAPTER ONE

The End

I knew that Ed had been stressed out and that his chest pain was bad, but we both thought that it was increasing pain from the esophageal spasms which had plagued his life for the last nine years. That week we had hired some heavy equipment to dig into the hill in back of our house and move the dirt to a low spot the other side of trees about 100' further back. It would allow for more space for better landscaping near the house. We were fixing up our 14 acre horse farm to sell in a few years. As usual with projects, it turned out to be a much larger and more expensive than we had expected. Ed being in charge of our building and landscaping projects as well as our finances could easily get upset if things were out of control. In spite of that, with an A1 personality, he was always dreaming up new projects and adventures. It was exciting being married to him as there was always something new. But he also added to his stress by insisting that everything had to be done right.

It was the beginning of May. Besides this big landscaping project, two weeks earlier, we had been in Florida shopping to buy a building lot for winter living in retirement in five or six years. We also had a 37' boat for ocean cruising which needed work before being launched the end of May. Having bought the boat secondhand the year before, Ed loved it and spent a lot of time cleaning and fixing it up. And we had a cabin on a lake in Maine which we would be soon be opening for the summer. We had built the cabin ourselves by working every weekend in the summer of 1987. Our plans for retirement were to sell the farm, live in Maine in the summer and go to Florida for the winter. We had dreams of lots of boating in Florida with trips to the Bahamas as well as coastal cruising.

Being the main maintenance and handyman for all our things, Ed had a lot on his mind. And the stress of the landscaping project turned out to be the straw that broke the camel's back.

Nine years earlier, Ed began having bouts of severe chest pain which he always described as being slightly on the right side of his chest and feeling like Charlie horse muscle spasms. He never had any other symptoms of heart disease like sweating or nausea. He bought several books on controlling heart disease through life style changes and followed one book religiously. By walking 4 to 6 miles a day and following a very low fat diet, he went from 270 lbs to 200 lbs. Being 6'4" tall, he looked great.

Having found out that the author of his favorite heart disease book was an internist at Massachusetts General Hospital, Ed got an appointment and began going to Boston, a 50 mile drive, for his healthcare. After doing some tests, the doctor assured Ed that his problems were not his heart but were digestive and connected to GERD, gastrointestinal reflux disease. And later when Ed's esophagus and stomach were examined through a scope, the specialist actually saw esophageal spasms happening. They do not really know the cause of esophageal spasms and there is no real cure, but the pain can normally be controlled by taking nitroglycerin and long acting nitrates, the same way angina is controlled.

Ed continued to go to this internist in Boston every six months for checkups with detailed blood tests and EKGs. Since he was also on one of the cholesterol lowering drugs, he had to be checked regularly for possible side effects. In the last year, Ed's esophageal spasms were generally getting worse and were really interfering greatly with his life. He suspected that they were related to the types of foods he ate. In January for two weeks before seeing the doctor, he went on a strict diet of lean meats and a lot of fresh fruits and vegetables, and he found that the chest pains disappeared almost entirely. He and the doctor were greatly encouraged. But after that, he could not keep on such a strict diet and the spasms got worse and worse. I kept suggesting that he go back to the doctor to see if there was anything, new or experimental, that could be done. But he was too stubborn to go back.

So that week the beginning of May when the heavy equipment was working and costing so much, Ed was very stressed with a lot of chest pains. On Thursday evening, when I got home from work, our backyard was totally torn up but was in the final stages before being all smoothed over. On driving out to the grocery store for food for dinner and for a nitroglycerin refill, I suggested that instead I drive Ed directly into Boston to the emergency room. He refused, probably because of the unfinished project in our backyard. We agreed though that, once the equipment was out of our yard on Friday, we would drive up to the place in Maine and do nothing but relax for the weekend.

On Friday, I left work a little early and got home at 5pm expecting to drive to Maine. The heavy equipment was out of there. Ed had gotten the bill about an hour before. Instead of being busy getting ready to leave for Maine, Ed was sitting in the living room in the rocking chair. He apologized for not getting anything done and not even feeding our two dogs. He said that his chest had been bothering him too much. I said no problem and suggested having a light dinner, relaxing for the evening and going up to Maine in the morning.

A few minutes after 7pm, we were in the living room watching the beginning of a movie on the DVD player when Ed turned to me and said he thought he was passing out. I immediately ran to the kitchen wall phone and called 911.

I could still see him from the kitchen and saw that he was going through some contortions. I don't know how long it was before the paramedics got there but I would guess five to ten minutes. They said that they felt a weak pulse and worked on him for a while before putting him in the ambulance. I stood back just watching, in shock, and not quite comprehending what I was watching. They offered to have me ride in the ambulance to the hospital. But not knowing how I would get home, I followed the ambulance in my car. I was alone and did not know if there would be anyone to drive me home.

Deep inside, I knew that Ed had died as the ambulance was not going fast and did not have its sirens going. But being in denial as most people would have been, I did not allow myself to really think that way. After all, things always work out for the best, don't they?

Ed and I had been married for almost 34 years with a marriage that seemed to get better each year. We fell in love essentially at first site and were true soulmates. We just loved being together no matter whether it was for an evening of television or for one of the many adventures we shared. We had friends, but since we were so close, we did not socialize a lot. We never had children but through the years had many horses, dogs and cats. We had no close family members.

When the ambulance got to the hospital, I followed as they took Ed into a room. A nurse approached me and said that I should wait in a waiting room down the hall. And a few minutes later, a doctor came in and told me that Ed had died.

A nurse asked if I had any family to call. I said "No, but there is one friend I want to call." My friend, Beth, had kept her horse at my place until I had sold my last horse three years before. She was normally out with her husband on Friday evenings, but luckily that Friday, she was home. Of course, she was shocked when she got my call and said that she would drive right down.

While I waited for Beth, I went in with Ed to say "Good-Bye." He was lying on a table with a tube coming out of his mouth which had probably been put in by the paramedics. I held his hand and told him that I would always love him and that it had been "quite a party." We had done a lot and had some great times together. I could not have had a more exciting life. We had been big fans of the mini-series, *Lonesome Dove*, and loved the line when Gus was dying and said that it had been "quite a party." I knew Ed would have agreed. We both thought alike. I did not cry. I am told that I would have been in shock and could not comprehend what was happening. Being in a situation like this can only be described as surreal.

I was glad to have Beth arrive and be with me while we waited for a social worker and the state medical examiner to arrive, which I assumed was standard procedure. Since everything was a blur, I do not really know when everything happened, but I think the social worker got there by 8:30 and the medical examiner was not there for at least another hour. The medical examiner seemed pretty sure that Ed had a heart attack. But since I was only aware of issues with esophageal spasms and not the heart, I requested that an autopsy be done. The medical examiner agreed and filled out the paperwork to have the autopsy done the next day.

I got the autopsy results in a phone call a few days later and in writing 5 or 6 weeks later. The doctor told me the Ed had moderate to severe cardiovascular disease with two major arteries to the heart 90% clogged. He had never had a stress test. She also said that this would have begun many years before, possibly in his twenties. He was 57 when he died.

Ed had been a big, strong, dynamic man who never liked being dominated by anyone and who wanted to do things his way. If he had a choice, he would have wanted to die exactly as he did, fast and painlessly. It was just a few years too early. Even though I am sure that afternoon he had suspected something serious was wrong, he never wanted to go to the emergency room. He did it his way.

Over the course of the next year or two, I went through a lot of second guessing as to what I should have done differently or what could have been done differently. I thought about the night before when I wanted to drive him into Boston, but if I had without his consent, he might have had a heart attack in the car on the highway. If he had gotten to a hospital, maybe he could have had bypass surgery. But that does not always go smoothly or easily. Ed would not have liked being laid up. Then I would think about the autopsy results that said he had moderate clogging of his cerebral arteries. That meant to me that in a few years, he could very likely be a stroke victim. Ed would have considered a stroke to be about the worst thing that could happen. Then I had to consider the fact that Ed did have the esophageal spasms which were by themselves becoming more debilitating.

In the long run considering everything, I have come to realize that I could not live for Ed. I think that afternoon he suspected he was in bad shape and he never called 911. Things happened as they did and I cannot change anything. I have learned to accept what happened and not beat myself up for not doing anything differently. I think it is totally normal to question the "What if's", but nothing will change the outcome. I was not the first person to lose my husband and I definitely was not the last. I had to learn how to go on.

CHAPTER TWO

How to Continue?

The next few days I was in shock. I did not cry until Monday morning when the sympathy cards began to come. I tried to remember things Ed and I had talked about through the years and how Ed would want me to act. I kept telling myself that I had to be strong and independent.

Ed and I had developed a relationship of mutual understanding. We would spend hours discussing any and every subject, from our innermost thoughts to the latest book Ed was reading. Our thinking was almost always in agreement. Ed was an avid reader, and through his reading, he had learned a great deal about life and the nature of man. Now in my despair, I kept reminding myself of some Ed's favorite sayings and philosophies.

We learned a lot about aging and death from the lives of our parents. Ed's father was a research chemist who had gotten cancer and passed away in 1978 at the age of 62. His mother became very bitter about life since her husband had been taken away before enjoying retirement. She ended up having a fatal heart attack in 1980 at the age of 60. Ed and I realized that the spouse who dies first would want to think of their loved one proceeding with life and not becoming so bitter. Ed's father was known to have many bits of wisdom and often used to say "Something good comes out of everything." Through his death, he gave us a much greater understanding of life and death.

My parents had longevity but did not have much quality of life for their last 10 to 12 years. My father had just passed away at 92 a little more than a year before Ed. My mother was still alive but had Alzheimer's disease and could not even recognize her own family. She passed away a few months after Ed at the age of 88. The last few years of their lives were spent in a nursing home in the same room, starring and nitpicking at each other. After about age 80, my father frequently said "These golden years aren't what they are cracked up to be." He had lost his balance and had to use a cane or walker, which had to be a hard adjustment considering in his 70's he had been walking five to six miles a day. Ed commented many times that his parents had died young, but there is something to be said for not having to go through what my parents were experiencing.

As I tried to get through the first little while after Ed's death, I kept reminding myself that Ed was certainly right about dying young and that I needed to be strong and proceed with life. I also knew that Ed's life had been hindered greatly by the esophageal spasms which had no real cure. Even if he had gotten to the hospital for bypass surgery, he still would have been debilitated by his esophageal problems. I suspected that was why he did not want to go to the emergency room that afternoon. I remembered that in the past he had told me that the esophageal spasms were so bad a few times that he had even considered shooting himself to end them. He was not suicidal, but the thoughts had crossed his mind. Our marriage had been built on mutual love and respect, and I knew that I had to respect what I believed to be his decision.

I had many different thoughts as I tried to handle the grief and the feeling that I could not go on without Ed. I felt badly that, before this, I had not been able to sympathize with friends and relatives who had lost a loved one. But I also realized that the loss of a husband or wife or best buddy was different from some loses since everything in your life just stops. Any plans for the future all stop. Goals for retirement no longer fit for just you. You are alone and no longer have your best buddy to do things with. And for me as for many widows losing my husband meant that I had to sell my house and move as soon as possible. I was not capable of taking care of our horse farm alone. Maybe I felt this more than most without having any children to lean on, but I think the practical side of a relationship has to hit everyone.

However unlike many people, I was never mad and upset with Ed. I have just loved and missed him terribly. As part of the grieving process, I understand that people normally go through a stage of being upset and mad with their deceased loved one. I knew his innermost feelings and could never be mad with him for dying.

Overall, given the circumstances of Ed's death, I was thankful for several things. I was glad I had been with him to know that he did not suffer in his final moments. I was glad that he had not experienced a stroke or any long debilitating disease. The shock of having him die suddenly of a heart attack was hard to accept, but in the long run, I think it was best for both of us. And I was also glad that we had always appreciated each other and often said "I love you." As the saying goes, we had tried to take time to smell the roses and enjoy every day. There was nothing I wished I had said before his death. I had no regrets.

Neither of us was religious and neither of us believed in life after death. We both believed that when you are dead, you are dead and nothing else. But once Ed was dead, it was hard to accept the finality of not having him with me.

We had been brought up in Protestant churches but had never found anything satisfying in going to church. We became even more dissatisfied with religions as we saw family members become Born-Again Christians. They preached that their way was the only way to get to Heaven but they never changed their lives and often did not treat people decently. They ignored the Golden Rule and would say "Good works do not get you to Heaven." This kind of thinking drove Ed and me even further away from formal religions. We knew that if man is to live peacefully in society, he will have to treat his fellow man as he would want to be treated.

However, Ed was not ignorant of religious philosophy as his reading through the years included the Bible and many philosophy books. But he never developed a belief in life after death or any organized religion. He once told a good friend who believed in life after death after losing her parents, "If you are right and there is life after death and if something happens to me, then I will come back and watch you in the bathroom!" My friends and I have had many good laughs about this, although now it probably is not a joke. When Ed was alive, he could always think up some humorous wisecrack, no matter how irreverent it might have been.

As a result, Ed had told me many times that if something happened to him, he did not want any funeral service or anyone praying over him. I agreed since that was my view as well. We also agreed that we both wanted to be cremated and have our ashes blown to the wind on a small, uninhabited island on the wilderness lake in Maine where we had built a waterfront cabin.

So as I went through the painful task of contacting friends and relatives of Ed's death, I let them know that there would not be any service and that I would be distributing Ed's ashes privately later in the summer. I believe that some friends felt that without a ceremony they did not have closure, although the funeral home did have a website where people could enter condolences. And many did. Ed had always joked that he had no friends, but he was wrong. After his death, I found that he had many, many more than either he or I had realized. For the first few weeks after Ed's death, I was on the phone almost constantly with one friend or another. It was great to talk to people and it helped keep me sane.

For me, it was better not to have had the typical calling hours or funeral service. I don't think that I could have handled seeing Ed in a casket. I saw him to say good-bye in the hospital before Beth arrived. Other than that, I want to remember Ed as he was when he was alive.

Luckily, Beth insisted on accompanying me to the funeral home the next day to make the final arrangements which I knew Ed would have wanted to be as simple and inexpensive as possible. I was still in shock and found the whole experience bizarre. Knowing that I would be distributing Ed's ashes at the lake, I looked at wooden urns which would allow for easy distribution. They were in the $400-500 range and were only slightly bigger and nicer than the box that contained Grizz' ashes. Grizz was the big, black Australian Shepherd who died a few months before and who had been Ed's close buddy for almost 14 years. Grizz' box was included with his cremation. Not wanting to pay $400 for a box which would be thrown away eventually, I asked what Ed's ashes would be in if I paid nothing extra for a box. I elected to have the default cardboard box. So Grizz' ashes were in a box much better than Ed's, but I am sure that Ed would have said that was fitting since Grizz was more important. It was on our anniversary the end of August when I finally distributed both sets of ashes at the lake with a small group of friends and relatives present.

As time went on, I thought that I was handling the loss of my husband quite well, but as I look back on it I realize that my mind was mush even though I was accomplishing day to day tasks. I went back to work in my high pressure, high tech job after only a week and a half as I told myself that I should get back into a routine. Luckily, there was a temporary lull at work that allowed me to get by with less than optimal performance for a couple of months.

At home, I had the farm to maintain but everything seemed to be way more than I had the desire to do. I would look at the newly graded back yard with no grass and just think that I had to sell the place so I would not have to address the issues of making the place look decent. It was all full with things needed for hobbies, maintenance of cars and farm equipment and spare building materials left over from building all our buildings. I would walk out to the attached two car garage, look at the piles, pick up a spare part or two, get disgusted and walk back into the house. Gradually, I was able to address things one step at a time. It was a long process and it took me a year and a half to get rid of enough to sell the farm and move to a new single unit condo.

There were times when I wished that someone else would take care of everything, but I knew that I did not want that to happen either. The stuff was all part of the life that Ed and I had together. It was up to me to take care of this part of our lives.

I did not go to any bereavement group until one that was held for the holidays the following winter. I did however make a special effort to get back in touch with many old friends by spending a lot of time on the phone and getting together with one friend or another. I believe that I inadvertently created my own support network of friends who kept me sane and very busy. I could not have gotten through the grieving process without my friends.

And I should also stress that I could not have gotten through my grief without my two Cairn Terriers, Mugsy and Red, who were always happy to be with me. They kept me in a routine between feeding and lots of walks. Mugsy was the older of the two and spent every night on the bed with me. Since I did not have Ed there, it was good to have Mugsy to keep me company. They were not watch dogs, but they would let me know if someone was approaching the house. They saved me from having my imagination run away with me after dark.

Of course as I worked to handle my grief, I spent lots of time thinking about the life I had with Ed and how great he was. We had a great marriage with many adventures.

CHAPTER THREE

Reflections

As time went on, I knew that I had to get my act together and take care of business. I could not just wallow in grief and self pity.

The biggest thing was our small horse farm which we had built and developed ourselves over a period of years. In 1976, we bought a 14 acre piece of wooded land on a dirt road in a country town in New Hampshire. We had been living in a development near an interstate highway with lots of noise and we wanted to build a place for a few horses with privacy, peace and quiet. Our intent was to build a small house and barn where we could be self sufficient, if needed, and could keep two or three horses. We intended to do most of the work ourselves and have only a small mortgage. We cut down the trees ourselves and hired heavy equipment to grade the 500' driveway and the areas for the house, garage and barn. Somehow through the years, the property kept on growing to include not just the house which was a chalet with a large deck on front but also the two car garage, the three car garage, the barn, a half acre fenced riding ring behind the barn and an acre field behind the riding ring. Even though I did not have horses anymore, there was a lot to take care of. In the winter, the 500' driveway which snaked through woods and up a hill required major snow blowing and constant attention. In the summer, the grass needed almost constant attention.

The two of us could barely keep up with everything. Ed had done all the snow blowing and mowing. I knew I had to try to keep up with the mowing and keep the place looking somewhat respectable. For the next few months, I spent almost every evening after work doing an hour or two of mowing or weed eating. And in the time that I was not mowing, I had to start to try to figure out how to move out of the place before winter. They say that someone should not make any major decisions for a year after losing a spouse, but there was no doubt in my mind that I had to get out of that farm. The only problems were that I had to clean out all the buildings of 27 years worth of accumulated stuff and that I did not know what town or what type of house I wanted. In July feeling totally overwhelmed, I realized that I would have to spend the winter there by myself so I proceeded to have the driveway widened to allow me to hire someone to plow from the foot of the driveway. I also contracted to have projects done to make it ready for resale, like having a new roof on the house.

The good thing about all the mowing that spring and summer was that it was mindless work and it gave me a lot of time to reflect on my life with Ed. Keeping busy with work like that helped to keep me sane and not become too obsessed with grief.

Ed was a true Renaissance man. The dictionary defines a Renaissance man as "a man who had diverse interests and expertise in a number of areas." That was Ed. As a result our lives were filled with one exciting adventure after another.

Before I knew Ed, for some reason I was always afraid of having my life turn into what was then the average American lifestyle of getting married, having kids and gossiping over the back fence. In the first few weeks of knowing Ed, I soon came to the conclusion that my life would not be average with Ed. That turned out to be very true. Essentially nothing in our lives turned out to be average. Even in death, Ed has been able to communicate to allow me to handle my grief and proceed with life.

When we were first married, Ed had just gotten out of the Navy and was going back to college to get his Bachelors degree in Business Administration in Aviation Management and his MBA in Finance. He had always loved airplanes and flew as a private pilot even though he ended up as a financial consultant for most of his life. He also always loved anything that burned gasoline, motorcycles, cars, sports cars, trucks and boats. He did all the maintenance on our vehicles, toys and most appliances. He loved working with his hands.

In the meantime, I always worked so we would have a steady paycheck to pay bills. I had a degree in Chemistry and had met Ed when we were working at a chemical company. Once we got married, we moved to Daytona Beach, FL, where Ed went to college and I taught high school. After Ed graduated from college, we moved to New Hampshire where I got into the computer industry, initially in software engineer and then in marketing. Ed was my biggest supporter, always making me feel like I could do anything.

Ed was never average. He had a zest and enthusiasm for life. He always challenged himself with new things to learn and new adventures whether hobbies, sports or professional endeavors. He was an avid reader of all kinds of subjects – philosophy, politics, history and fiction. I always learned tons from him as he would discuss books with me after he read them.

In 1976, Ed ran for US Congress but soon became disenchanted with politics since he was more of a philosopher than politician. At that time, he concentrated his reading on books about libertarian philosophy. He was particularly impressed with one book by Albert Jay Nock that explained the idea that the only way any person can improve society is by presenting society with "one improved unit." It was after reading Nock that Ed started hoping that he would loose the election. And by a strange turn of events, he did. The following year, Ed submitted a brief resume with an article to be published and highlighted his goal in life to "Present society with one improved unit, nothing more, nothing less." In later years, Ed never talked much about this, but he truly did live life as one improved unit. He was considerate and decent to everyone and tried not to infringe on anyone else's rights. He didn't care what people did for a living or what kind of education they had.

Ed was a big believer in individual freedoms, free enterprise and limited government. When he was younger, he was known to pass out books to friends on freedom and liberty. As he got older, he became more cynical and realized the true nature of man and government would make it impossible to stop government from getting bigger. As Ed said many times, elected politicians are only a mirror image of the voters. If the average citizen does not know or care about the difference between right and wrong, then politicians will not either.

As time went on, Ed went from campaigning for Congress, to being campaign manager for a couple of candidates for US Senate, to donating to campaigns and to doing nothing more than voting and presenting society with one improved unit.

Through the years of building the horse farm, Ed's ingenuity was tested many times. He often quoted his father who used to say, "There is a solution to everything." And Ed would search until he found a solution to what was needed at the time. When we were building the farm house and later the cabin in Maine, he built tool sheds first so we could camp out while framing the buildings. During the construction of the farm house, I had quit my job for a few months and treated the time as a vacation.

Camping out and watching the construction activities turned out to be a great adventure. The first obstacle was what to do with Ed's business phone. He did not want it to be disconnected for the transition period with no new number for referral. Ed requested that the phone company install a phone in a box on a tree. He was able to hook up his answering system to inform people that no one was in the office at the present time (this was before automated voicemail). Next Ed built a single hole bench to serve as an outhouse and put it behind a pile of firewood. It had woods on the other three sides so it was private, but a little wet during a storm. Then he built a 7x10' tool shed which we used initially as our living room with chairs and a TV. Electricity was obtained by running extension cords from the temporary electrical service in front of the building site.

When we built the cabin in Maine, Ed orchestrated the project in a similar way, except this time he built a frame for a queen sized bed in the tool shed for extra comfort. He put the frame about 3' high so he could store tools underneath.

From the very first year together, we loved having dogs and cats. We had both grown up in families with cats so we always had at least one or two. But dogs were new to Ed. As

I have told many people through the years, "Ed never liked dogs until he met me." This sounds funny, but Ed's affection for dogs started from the beginning of our marriage. We always had at least two dogs at a time usually with one being a large dog and one being a small terrier. Sometimes when one dog was getting old, we would get a third and have the older dog help train the new puppy. Ed was always closest to the larger dogs with his last "true love" being the Australian Shepherd, Grizz, who died a few months before Ed. I think that part of Ed died with Grizz.

When we had horses on our small farm, they became more like backyard pets than barn animals. Even though horses were my passion, Ed loved them as well and was willing to help with their care. I owe Ed a lot for contributing as much as he did for my hobby, the horses.

Our marriage was based on love, communications and trust. I knew what he was experiencing and he knew what I was experiencing. We were always in lock step and operated as a team. Considering careers, hobbies and adventures, one decision we readily made was not to have children. And neither of us ever regretted it. We had an unconventional but a loving family made up of ourselves, horses, dogs and cats.

As I worked on mowing and doing other chores to maintain the farm after Ed's death, I thought about the events of our lives, the work, the laughter with the good times and perseverance with the hard times. Even in sad times, Ed had the ability to make a comment or crack a joke to break the ice and get everyone in the room laughing. Very often, laughter is the best medicine.

I remembered how he decided to write western novels, initially by ghost writing several. He was enchanted by the times in the old west and secretly wished he had lived a hundred years earlier when man could truly be free. When he did publish his own western novel, he set up a publishing company and learned how to work in the publishing industry.

For many years, Ed taught college level finance and economics, mainly in night school and changed the lives of many of students. Shortly after he died, I exchanged emails with a student he had taught in 1976 who said, "The introduction Ed gave me to Economics and especially to the Foundation for Economic Education led me to take up the personal study of Economics. I became an expert on libertarian ideology." I was always amused by Ed's trick to demonstrate to his Economics students about the true nature of redistribution of income by redistributing their grades. The better students quickly decided that they did not like giving points from their scores to the lesser students.

Ed and I accomplished a lot together. I realized that much of what made Ed unique were his written and verbal communication skills, his willingness to take on any challenges and his ability to figure out solutions. I did not know it at the time but these were some of the skills that must have contributed to allowing him to communicate with me after death.

While I worked on the various maintenance projects, I also would spend time thinking about my family. I tried not to, but it did cross my mind as I had been quite close with my parents in my younger years.

My father passed away at age 92 a little more than a year before Ed and my mother passed away of Alzheimer's disease at age 88 the day after I distributed Ed's ashes. The last few years they were alive were spent in a nursing home where my younger brother, Dick, put them without considering their feelings or preferences. He also refused to discuss the situation with myself or my older brother, Brien. Dick and his wife several years before had swayed my parents into making them trustees and executors of the two estates, even though they were totally irresponsible with money and, unbeknown to my parents, they had claimed bankruptcy a few years before. Immediately after putting my parents in the nursing home, Dick and his wife began spending my parents' money for themselves and moved into my parents' condo after making renovations. They maintained that my father was approving everything.

Observing some of this financial abuse and suspecting more, I requested that my brother produce accountings as required by New Hampshire law of any fiduciary. When he refused to do these accountings, I petitioned probate court to require the accountings to the letter of the law. The whole situation got really ugly. Dick viciously turned my parents, my older brother and sister against me. The court case lasted for a year and a half with a judge who did not care and never appeared to have read any documents between hearings. Even though the judge initially ordered that these accountings be done to probate court standards, we never got accountings that conformed to the standards. But the judge was not fazed by this lack of a proper accounting. After more than a year, the judge began pushing for us to go into mediation as it appeared she did not want to handle the case any longer. My first reaction was "How do you mediate an accounting which was never produced?" But after my father passed away a few months later, I gave in and consented to the mediation. We ended up negotiating to have my brother and his wife removed from all fiduciary responsibilities. And since they wanted to move back to Texas where they had lived before, my two brothers and my sister negotiated to have my mother moved to a nursing home in California near my sister. They did not want my mother near me.

As a result of all this, my relationship with my parents was at rock bottom by the time they passed away. Luckily my mother, who I had been very close to in earlier years, did not really know what was happening.

Ed was very supportive of me through this whole ordeal. But unfortunately, the rest of my family seemed to blame Ed for a lot of the upheaval with most of them exhibiting pure hatred for Ed. As a result, I did not call anyone in my family after Ed died as I knew they would be glad and gloating. I ended up telling my older brother, Brien, almost four months later when he called to tell me that my mother had died.

Without being conscious of it, the difficulties in life created by my family situation which happened at almost the same time as losing my husband contributed to my need to develop a greater understanding of life. Through several years of reading and help from Ed, I changed and developed spiritually, not religiously. All the members of my family are Born Again Christians. Observing their conduct in life showed me that religion does not help someone to be loving and compassionate.

CHAPTER FOUR

Friends & Initial Signals

The week after Ed's death, his sister, Dorothy, came from Toronto to support me. Without an actual ceremony to plan and prepare for, I was not surrounded by the usual activity involving a funeral. But I kept busy on the phone almost constantly with old friends and relatives. It was these conversations that helped get me through the initial shock. I did not plan it, but I inadvertently had begun the first baby step on the path to healing.

One of the calls was from an old friend who I had not seen in several years. She was able to understand my shock and feelings since a number of years before she had lost her eleven year old son when he was hit by a truck coming home from sledding. Among other things, she told me that there would be things that will happen in the house, electronic things, like the microwave beeping when it is not supposed to. And she added, "Don't worry, that will be Ed." I thanked her for the comforting words, but I was pretty skeptical. I told Dorothy after getting off the phone and we both had a good chuckle.

The manager of the marina where our big Sea Ray was stored had suggested that I call a woman who also had a big boat at the marina and who had been faced with the same situation five years before. Her husband had died suddenly of a heart attack leaving her with a big boat. Even though she had not known how to handle it, she had decided to keep the boat and learn how to captain it. A half hour after hearing that Ed would be causing strange things to happen, I called her even though we had not met. In the course of our conversation, the phone line beeped very loudly three times. Each time it interrupted our talking. After the second time, I asked if there was something wrong with her phone but she said that she had never heard that sound before. I was on my kitchen phone, the one I had been using constantly. I had never heard it beeping and did not think it was my phone. When I got off the phone, I told Dorothy. We both laughed and jokingly said at the same time, "That must be Ed!" I later learned that talking on the phone about selling Ed's prize boat would often get a reaction, but more on that later.

From the beginning when Beth tried to console me, she would tell me that she was sure that, if anyone were going to communicate after death, it would be Ed because we were so close. I felt appreciative that she would say such a thing, and would tell her that I wished she was right, but I did not believe it.

Another friend, Cathy, who had gone through a lot of grieving after her father died a few years before, sent me a book of daily meditations and sayings which turned out to help me tremendously in the first few months. Cathy also stuck into the book a separate photocopied page of the following passage:

Death is nothing at all, I have only slipped away into the next room. I am I and you are you. Whatever we were to each other that we still are. Call me by my old familiar name; speak to me in the easy way which you always used. Put no difference in your tone; wear no forced air of solemnity or sorrow. Laugh as we always laughed at the little jokes together. Play, smile, think of me. Let my name be ever the household word that it always was. Let it be spoken without effort, without a trace of a shadow in it. Life means all that it ever meant. It is the same as it ever was. There is unbroken continuity. Why should I be out of mind because I am out of sight? I am waiting for you for an interval, somewhere very near, just around the corner. All is well!

Michael T. Foley, MD
12/08/02

At the bottom of the page, Cathy added the following note:

Diana,

I read this passage time and again and it helps me realize that physical body is only part of the relationship we hold with the ones we love. Our relationships run to a depth far deeper and you will find that Ed will be there for you in one way or another time and again (and when you need him) forever. It is different but it is real. Cathy

For months, reading this passage would bring tears to my eyes even though these were new concepts for me. The idea that I should be talking to Ed the same as ever was a novel idea. With nothing to lose by trying, I began talking to Ed as though he was still with me and found a new comfort. I now realize that I was being led to the next baby step on the path to healing.

Once I went back to work, I found tremendous support from many co-workers. One memorable comment was from an Indian Hindu guy whom I greatly respected. He told me that he knew that Ed was in a better place and that Ed had a lot of good karma. I thanked him for the nice words and told him that I hoped he was right. But I never did understand how anyone could be going to a better place when they die and I did not know anything about karma. I have later learned how true these kind words are.

Even though I did not believe my friends when they suggested Ed was still with me and would be sending me signals, a part of me wanted to believe he was real and with me. I began to try to notice any unexplained events which might be Ed. I was skeptical and tried to explain everything away. But at the same time, each event gave me a warm feeling of comfort. As time went on, I found my belief that Ed was around me became stronger and stronger until, in September, I finally declared, "I am a believer."

Initially, I thought that lights were either turned on or turned off differently from how I had left them. But I could not definitely determine if what I was seeing was true.

As time went on, my work life settled into more of a routine. But at home my life was in chaos between figuring out how to maintain the farm and do things like getting grass planted after the new grading done the week before Ed's death. My mind was mush and I could barely function. I knew it was spring, everything was growing and everything needed to be cut. I had to learn how to use Ed's tools and the power equipment. I was not afraid of running the equipment, but I was afraid of having something breakdown. Ed was my mechanic. I had no idea how to fix things, and I did not have a friend nearby who I felt comfortable in asking for help.

Being totally overwhelmed by the farm maintenance, all I could think about was how soon I could sell and buy a condo. About two weeks after Ed's death, one of my neighbors came over with a friend who was a possible buyer. While the three of us were walking around the property, we noticed that in the trees in front of the house there were three male Scarlet Tanagers, all on branches within about a hundred feet of each other. Scarlet Tanagers are extremely rare birds. During the spring, the male is a brilliant orange/red with black wings. Other years, I considered myself lucky to see one of these beautiful birds once or twice in a season. I would always remark to Ed about such a sighting as we both enjoyed seeing wild birds. But seeing three of these birds at the same time is essentially unheard of. Looking back on that happening now, I am sure that Ed somehow created the event and wanted to let me know he was with me while I was trying to sell our farm. At the time, I felt warm inside with the idea that Ed was with me, but I was not convinced.

A few days before going to the cabin in Maine the end of May, I decided to tackle a couple of small projects using Ed's tools. I started charging the boat battery for the small boat in Maine on Ed's workbench. I was not sure if I had it set up correctly since I had never done it before. I was frustrated that I had no one to ask for help. I then went to the barn with a few tools to see if I could fix the hand pump we used for the dug well in back of the barn. I soon needed a different tool and went back to the garage. On entering the garage, I began looking for the right tool, but noticed that the wall clock above the workbench was ticking loudly as it had never done before. It had not even been working before. The clock had been a gift from my parents and neither Ed nor I had ever liked it. I realized that this would be a unique way for Ed to use to get my attention and to let me know he was watching over me especially while I was using his tools. We used to joke about how much Ed loved his tools.

I know he would have been proud of me and would have been cheering me on. The next morning, I called Beth and told her, "Maybe I am becoming a believer."

Off and on after that, the clock would sometimes tick loudly but make no noise the rest of the time. Once at the end of that summer, I was using Ed's compressor and noticed that the clock was ticking loudly but was stuck on one time. I felt a new measure of confidence as I knew Ed was probably helping me use his tools.

Once a couple of months after Ed's passing when I came into the garage, I found that there were three things next to Ed's workbench which had not been there before. The three things were a wide, 90 degree joint of PVC pipe, a roll of brown wrapping paper and a power jigsaw. I do not know where these things were before, but they were not next to the workbench. I don't even think there was any wrapping paper in the garage. The closest wrapping paper was in Ed's office in the house. I soon realized the significance of this mix of things. A couple of weeks before Ed's death we had been in Florida and put an offer on a lot of land which was at the corner of streets named Jigsaw and Cone. Of all of Ed's tools, it was no coincidence that it was a jigsaw that got moved. And I think that the wrapping paper and the PVC pipe were things that could be used to make a cone.

Another time I noticed that three cans of paint that I had put down on the floor were put back on the shelf. The signals from Ed seemed to be strongest in the garage since he loved his tools and workshop so much.

Another place where I felt Ed's presence was his office. He had been the financial consultant who kept his office in shape and who was very particular about doing business correctly. He had even kept our personal finances on Peachtree Accounting software so that he could print checks on a laser printer and print balance sheets and reports. And of course, he also had his publishing company maintained as a Peachtree business. He used to tell me that I should learn to use Peachtree as I would be in bad shape if something happened to him. A few weeks after his death needing to pay bills, I sat down to figure it out. It took me almost two days but I did it. I know that Ed was watching and helping. I felt pretty proud of myself for becoming proficient with Peachtree.

Ed had kept an extra office chair next to his desk where one of the dogs, Red, always slept while he was working. Red continued to get in that chair whenever I was at the desk. But there would be times when she would refuse to get in the chair. I began feeling that Ed was there instead. Red is a very sensitive dog and frequently acted very differently that summer. I suspected that Ed would talk through the dogs to let me know when he was there.

I have always taken the dogs out for a short walk in the evening before going to bed. Before Ed passed away, if Ed was upstairs in the bedroom when I came in, Red would come back into the house all excited and would run up the stairs to greet Ed enthusiastically. She would act as if she had not seen him in a long time, even though it had only been a few minutes. After Ed's passing, most of the time she would not be excited when she came back in the house, but once in a while she would wag her tail crazily and run up the stairs to find Ed but then could not. I have suspected that Ed created scents or noises that Red could smell or hear so she would run to greet him. I was always glad to think that Ed might be around.

In September, the toner cartridge for the ten year old laser printer ran out. I felt I needed to keep this printer going as I did not want to set up another printer to print checks from Peachtree. So I took the cartridge to Staples to buy a new one which had to be ordered. And trying to be real efficient, I dumped the old one into the used bin at Staples. When the new one came in, I went to work installing it in the printer. After some fiddling, I realized that I had taken out and thrown away the whole developer unit as well as the toner cartridge. So I had to go back and order a developer unit which cost far more than the printer was worth. While I was trying to figure out how to put the toner cartridge in the printer without the developer unit, Red was under the desk terrified and shaking. She had never acted this way in the office before. However a few days later when I was installing the new developer unit and the new toner cartridge correctly, Red was totally relaxed. I believe that the first evening when Red was upset, Ed was there watching me mess up his printer. His frustrations must have terrified Red with the negative energy.

Another time in the office, I got email from one of Ed's airport friends who told me of the death of another airport buddy who Ed may have known. The guy left his wife in a similar situation to mine with lots of things and unfinished projects. I wrote back a fairly lengthy email and then turned off the computer to get ready for work. This particular morning while I was getting ready for work both dogs acted strangely. They both stayed close to me. Red was scared and would not come into the bedroom without a lot of encouragement. Those emails seemed to have gotten quite a reaction from Ed.

As I wrote earlier, Ed had been plagued with esophageal spasms for the last nine years of his life. He always described them as feeling like Charlie horse muscle spasms in his chest. They would usually be completely debilitating until they subsided. Throughout that first summer after his death, I frequently would get Charlie horses in one calf or the other for only five to ten seconds at a time. They would happen most often in the early morning when I was first waking up. Since I rarely had ever gotten Charlie horses before, I started to suspect that Ed was trying to signal when he was with me.

One Saturday morning the end of the summer, I decided that I did not need the post office box which Ed had maintained for the publishing company. So I gathered the keys and headed to the post office to discontinue the box. But on my way to the post office (3.5 miles away), I got a severe Charlie horse in my left calf that would not stop.

Suspecting that Ed did not want me to stop the publishing company, I finally said into the air that I would keep the box. By the time I got to the post office, the Charlie horse was gone. I think that Ed knew that I was destined to write this book.

I kept the big boat that Ed loved so much. All summer, I had hired a captain to go with me and train me on boat handling. But it was getting awfully expensive. So in September, I listed the boat for sale with a broker. The next week I was on the phone with an old friend and told him that I was selling the boat. In the course of our conversation, the phone line beeped several times. This was the same thing that had happened in May when I was talking about selling the boat. A few days later, I was on the phone with some friends from the marina and I was saying that I might get out of boating all together. At that point, there were three successive, loud beeps which came from the living room and not from the phone line. At first I thought it was the smoke detector but then I realized it was not the same sound. The next day I figured out that it was the handheld phone in the living room which was beeping as though someone had hit the button on the home unit to find the handset. The home unit was on a table where the dogs could not have touched it. I knew there was no explanation for this beeping other than it had been caused by Ed.

This episode of beeping was the point when I became a believer with no reservations. With all the rest of the signals, I had continued to have doubts even though I was comforted with the thought that Ed might be there. Ed had persisted in practically hitting me on the side of the head all summer with signals to get my attention. After this event, I knew that Ed was definitely still alive in spirit and with me.

CHAPTER FIVE

Research

A fter becoming a believer when I talked about getting
out of boating and immediately heard beeping
sounds in the living room, I decided that I had to do my
own research into life after death. This idea was all new
to me. Being a scientist, I did not want to believe the first
concepts I stumbled upon. I wanted to read and research
the spiritual world from many perspectives and determine
the beliefs that made the most sense to me. After reading
in the neighborhood of seventy to eighty books, attending
seminars presented by famous mediums and talking with
many people, I found myself seeing similar, if not the same,
information described from different points of view.

Some books pointed out that people who have had near
death experiences often do a lot of research into life after
death and investigation into many of the world's religions,

but they do not end up in any one religion. Even though I did not have a near death experience, I feel I was given a similar jolt by never believing in life after death, losing my husband and finding out for certain that he is still alive and with me. Even now, I am still reading and researching from many perspectives and am now studying various religions. I do not believe that I will ever adopt any single religion.

Our spirits are basically electromagnetic energies or entities which exist in another dimension which we on earth do not really understand. Physicists have proven the existence of around eleven dimensions, so this is totally feasible. These entities have the abilities to travel at the speed of light and to observe and be with us in the physical world. We are supposed to be able to communicate with spirits not just by talking out loud but through our unspoken thoughts. Again physicists are doing a lot of research into the power of thinking and how thoughts can cause things to happen. I personally have had a number of times when I have thought something and have gotten an immediate sign that Ed and/or the spirit world heard.

On the skeptical side when I was first doing my research, I would ask myself how do we really know that the spirits are there since we cannot see them. Then I would remember when I taught high school chemistry, the students frequently would ask how do we really know that atoms and molecules are there. I would tell them that scientists have performed enough tests to determine the properties of atoms and molecules. And I would go on to point out that if you walked into a totally dark room and stepped into a bucket of water, you would not have to see it to know it was there. I think that knowing there are spirits around us is a similar situation. If you see and experience the effects of what they can do, then you can conclude they are there.

Initially in my research, one of my many friends already into new age reading gave me two of James Van Praagh's books, *Talking to Heaven* and *Healing Grief.* I loved these books and went on to read more books by mediums, then books by people describing near death experiences, books by doctors who had surveyed people who had near death experiences, books by psychiatrists who hypnotized people to find out about past lives and about life in between lives, books by people who had communications with past loved ones, books by people who can will out of body experiences, books about the power of thoughts and prayers, books about how your thinking influences your life and books about the world's religions. I have found myself gaining understanding and spirituality. While I have not totally accepted all the concepts and information, I have tried to stay open to the ideas. Having personally witnessed some amazing events, I have a hard time declaring that something cannot be possible.

One of the nicest books that I read in the first few months is one titled *Hello from Heaven* by Bill and Judy Guggenheim. The Guggenheims had interviewed several thousand people and had them describe the after death communications (ADCs) they had with their deceased loved ones. They then categorized similar experiences into chapters of quotes from many of the people. It is amazing how the descriptions from different people are almost the same. I am sure that they are not fabricated for the book, as I have personally had many similar experiences and I have talked to many friends and acquaintances who have also described similar events to the ones in the book.

My friend, Beth, had described to me a number of times how, once in a while when she is riding her horse in the woods, she will get the feeling of the spirit of her father totally surrounding herself and her horse. She knows that her horse feels it too as he acts differently. One chapter of *Hello from Heaven* quotes a number of people who have had the feeling of being totally surrounded by their loved ones. I was shocked with how similar Beth's description was to the ones in this book.

In another chapter of *Hello from Heaven,* titled "More than a Dream: Sleep-State ADCs," the Guggenheims say that clear, distinct dreams of a loved one are actual visitations the same as an apparition appearing in waking hours. I am personally convinced that they are right about this as I have had probably close to two dozen dreams where Ed has appeared clearly and distinctly to either send particular messages or send me his love telepathically. And one time I received an important message from our big dog, Grizz, who had passed away a few months before Ed. These dreams are very different from my normal dreams. From my experience, these dream visitations are controlled by the spirit world, since I have not been able to will their occurrence. Although I do have a friend who has told me that she has been able to focus on Ed before going to sleep and get messages from him in her dreams. The messages she received that way meant nothing to her but were meaningful to me. I will cover more about all these dreams later.

Another chapter in *Hello from Heaven* demonstrates how spirits will frequently send particular scents which their loved ones will identify with them, like the smell of roses or pipe tobacco. In my experiences, since Ed and I met in a chemistry lab, I have had the smells of organic solvents, such as rubbing alcohol or acetone, just materialize out of no where. These scents appeared a number of times when I was stressed out about something at work. I believe that Ed was trying to tell me to calm down.

Hello from Heaven also talks about how people frequently have a sign appear which is unique and confirms that their loved one is still living. Typical signs are butterflies, birds, rainbows, flowers and certain animals. Reading this reinforced my feeling that the appearance of three Scarlet Tanagers while I was showing our farm to prospective buyers a couple of weeks after Ed's passing were sent by Ed.

One of the self-help books that seemed particularly powerful to me was *The Power of NOW* by Eckhart Tolle. As the title says, it is all about living life in the NOW or the present. If you really focus on the current moment, you will realize that everything is fine and you are okay. But if you look forward or backward, you can get upset. I started to realize that was true for me. As long as I focused on the present moment, then I was okay without Ed. But if I allowed to think about the past, then I would get upset thinking about all the things that Ed and I had experienced. And if I thought about the future, then I would get upset thinking about the future without Ed. When I began a concerted effort not to think about the past or the future, my feelings of grief lessened.

Books by people who have had near death experiences or books summarizing interviews with adults and children who have had near death experiences describe the transition from passing away to crossing over almost exactly the same way. They say that the spirit will leave the body and often hover over his/her body watching what is going on without being able to communicate. Under normal circumstances, the spirit will soon see and be attracted to a bright white light, and will usually be met by deceased friends or close relatives who help with the transition. Shortly after this, the spirit will have a comprehensive life review which will reveal all their life's interactions with other people, good and bad. They all describe a beauty and a feeling of love and peace which they have never experienced before. Sometimes they see a loving spirit being who is believed to be Jesus, a Saint or another savior. And almost universally for near death experiences, people do not want to come back to this world. I now understand why, when someone passes, it is said that the deceased is in a better place.

Books by mediums give a lot of information about what it is like to communicate with the spirit world and what messages they have heard. They all stress that love is what ties us together. Even once spirits have crossed over, they can and usually do come back to watch over loved ones, especially when there is a particular need. Their love for us and their basic personalities do not change. A quote from the James Van Praagh BLOG for the TV show, Ghost Whisperer, on 3/2/06 states, "The spirit people are concerned about our daily lives and don't just cease to be!" I have also seen in an internet chat room with James Van Praagh where he said that spirits always come to their own funerals.

At the end of John Holland's book, *Born Knowing*, John has a number of commonly asked questions and answers. Here is one of them:

Q. Why do spirits come back?

A. Because they can. People on the Other Side want to share our lives with us. I've done many sittings where spirits acknowledge that they were around their loved ones during difficult times to lend their support and strength. However, they don't just visit when the going gets tough. I often receive evidence of spirits who were there to see their children get married or witness the birth of a baby. Holidays and special occasions are also big for them – they want to see us happy and like to take part in that joy. After all, if they were here physically, they'd be at such events. Being in spirit doesn't change the fact that they're still our family and still care about us.

I have become a big fan of the TV show, Ghost Whisperer, which has James Van Praagh as Executive Producer. The show is about a woman who has the ability to see and hear spirits who have not crossed over and who have stayed on earth for some reason. The star helps these earth bound spirits to cross over. But the impression that this TV show gives is that once a spirit goes to the light and crosses over, the spirit is gone and will not be heard from again. In a session on a cruise with James Van Praagh, I asked James why the show gave this impression. He said that this is Hollywood's portrayal for the dramatization effect and that he had to yield to Hollywood's marketing. He also added that he never actually communicates with spirits until after they have crossed over. I do not know why this is true, but I find it fascinating.

From my experiences, I also know that our loved ones are around us more than we realize. In the next chapter, I will describe events that lead me to know this is true.

Part of my understanding has also come from talking with friends and acquaintances. As my awareness increased, I made a habit of feeling people out about their knowledge or acceptance of life after death. As an informal tally, I have figured that approximately 75% of people have had experiences themselves, have heard of experiences or are open to the idea that things can happen. This predominance of people is surprising since very few people dare to talk about this subject.

Here are some of the experiences described to me by people who I believe to be just regular people with no supernatural capabilities.

Shortly after I began my research into life after death, I joined a bereavement group formed to help people through the holiday season. At the end of the first meeting, I struck up a conversation with another woman, Anna, who had lost her husband suddenly a couple of months after Ed had passed. We soon started talking about signals and communications from our husbands. She told me how she had seen her husband the first night after his passing. She said that she was staying at her daughter's house that night and had just gone to bed. She heard a knock at the door which she assumed was her daughter. She said to come in and the door pushed open. And then she saw her husband. He asked her if she was all right and then he disappeared. Anna also remembers that on their anniversary, she dreamed that her husband was in her bedroom leaning on her bureau. This time he told her that they would always be a pair. She also frequently has had other signals including smelling his pipe tobacco and feeling his touch on her shoulder.

I spent a week in Florida in a time share condo with a friend, her mother and another recent widow, Betsy. Betsy had lost her husband just two years before and had the experience of seeing her husband about ten days after he passed. He had given her the message that he loved her and he was all right. Since then she had other signals and feelings that her husband was around her. Interestingly, while we were talking about these things during that week in Florida, there were two times when the electricity in condo blinked off for about a minute each time. Afterward we learned of no real explanation for these outages. We suspected that it might have been caused by one of our husbands.

My friend, Cindy, who had lost her eleven year old son when he was hit by a truck coming home from sledding, told me of an amazing happening. About two weeks after her son passed, she finally found enough strength to leave the house and go out to her barn to work with her horses. While she was busy working, all of a sudden a young, blond, blue eyed man appeared almost out of nowhere. He asked her if she was all right and handed her a business card. She said yes, even though she wasn't, and continued working. A minute later, she turned to say something more but found he had disappeared without saying another word. She also did not see a car pull up or leave, but she admits that she really hadn't been looking. Later she looked at the man's business card (which she still has), and saw that his name was Christian S. Cumback. She did not think to call the number on the card until about two years later. She found that it was the number of a company of insurance investigators, but at that time, no one knew anything about a Christian S. Cumback.

One can wonder if this man was real, but even if he were, what were the chances that a man with such a name would stop on the first day she was out of her house and not say anything other than to ask if she was okay?

Another friend who had lost her father told of a time when her mother, Ruby, was out one night and got lost driving home. Being very upset, she stopped her car, started crying and yelled out for her husband to help her. Suddenly a big, black car drove up and stopped in back of her. A woman got out, came up to the car and offered to help. She told Ruby to follow her car and she would show her how to get home.

A good friend of Ed's, Chuck, was always skeptical when I would talk about some of my signals from Ed. However, a few weeks after his brother died of ALS, Chuck began to have some unexplainable things happen. The most amazing event happened one evening when he heard a noise in the garage. He looked into the garage and realized that his wife's car was sitting idling with no one around. The car also had no keys in it, the doors were locked and the headlights were on.

A close, Irish friend, Jo, has told me of going to the funeral of an elderly aunt. The day of the funeral in Ireland was cloudy and rainy. But just as they were at the graveside about to lower the casket into the ground, the sun came out and shone on the casket. Jo was pleased as she knew that would have been something her aunt would have done.

Bea, a friend in Connecticut, was always spiritual in her outlook on life and was very close with her dad. So it came as no surprise to her to see her father sitting in a chair in her spare bedroom shortly after he passed. And she frequently felt her father's presence around her house in spite of the fact that he had never lived there. She also remembers a time when she was in her basement and her small, Yorkshire Terrier started down the steps but took a misstep about halfway down and began falling. She says that miraculously it appeared that someone caught the dog in mid air and placed him carefully on the basement floor. She is sure that her father was there helping at this almost disastrous moment.

My cousin's wife, Linda, was also close with her father and has had a number of amazing events happen. At my request, she has written the following descriptions of these times:

1. While Dad was in the hospital the week he passed away, there was a profound presence in the room on the Sunday before the Tues. he passed away. My Mom and daughter went to run an errand. I was holding Jasmine in my arms sleeping (she was 7 months old), and Dad was asleep. I began to feel a very powerful

presence in the room that was SO PEACEFUL, it felt like Dad and Jasmine and God were all communicating---It was so Warm, Peaceful, powerful, full of Energy, very positive. Yet they were both sleeping. But something was sure going on at that moment, I was just in awe of it, and very aware that something very special was taking place at that moment.

2. Before Dad had passed away he was only able to wave to Jasmine from his chair.

    Several months after Dad passed away, my Granddaughter (who was 7 months old when he passed away) was sitting in my lap at Mom and Dad's house. Above the fireplace Mantel was his picture that we used at his Memorial. She looked up at it and waved the exact same way Dad had waved to her and said "Hi PAPA" This is not a name we would have referred to him by, it would have been "Grandpa Ted"----She had never heard anyone refer to him as "PAPA" This was definitely between Dad and Jasmine.

3. Jasmine would look up while playing and talk to "PAPA" on several occasions while still a baby/toddler.

4. Mom was getting into my car after picking her up one day. She chose to sit in the back seat with

Jasmine to be near her in the car seat. After she got in, Jasmine said to her (she was between twelve and eighteen months old.) with body language of surprise (leaning away from Mom and a very quizzical look on her face). "Why are you wearing PAPA's Coat????" Now Jasmine never saw my Dad in a coat ever. Mom did have a coat very similar to Dad's but this particular day Mom decided to wear Dad's coat---on a whim-- There was no way for Jasmine to have known this, or me in fact. It just gave us goose bumps all over!!! Good ones though. I still get them whenever I tell this story.

5. My husband was working shift work, so he was gone during the night. I kept hearing a noise in the middle of the night. I finally got up to see what the noise was. I found a Teddy Bear in the girls closet snoring. I just laughed at this, and said "you got me, Dad, your playing with me, aren't you?"

    My Dad's nickname was "Teddy Bear." When he was a toddler, he lived in a rooming house and was given that nickname by the ladies that also lived there. It stuck, but was shortened to Ted. He went by Ted all his life even though his real name was Charles.

6. This Teddy Bear was given to Jasmine on Christmas after Dad passed away. It would snore if laying down, with it's tummy going up and down and making the snoring sound. If sitting up it was **quiet.** If squeezed it laughed. When I found the Teddy Bear in the Closet **snoring** it was **SITTING UP**!!!!!! I believe with it being a Teddy Bear, Dad's name Ted, and the fact that <u>Dad loved to tease</u> ---this was a sign from him having fun with me. I just laughed and felt very warm and loved the fact he was playing with me in the middle of the night.

7. This one just happened this past Tues. Jan 9, 2007. I was on the computer before going to have a colonoscopy that morning. When all of a sudden a Snow Globe that is musical, started to play!!!! (It's been a couple of years since we wound it up at least) I immediately knew that Dad was with me and was going to be with me during the procedure. I went over and picked up the Snow Globe and kissed the Snow Globe and "thanked Dad for being with me, and said I loved him." It was so reassuring and I could feel his presence in the room with me.

I have read in a number of places that this is not an uncommon occurrence for deceased relatives to visit small children and establish a close relationship even from spirit form. Children are more sensitive to the presence of higher frequency beings than adults. It is also common that when spirits do appear, they show themselves in dress that was typical of them in life. So it is very likely that my cousin's granddaughter had seen her great grandfather in that coat.

When children talk about their imaginary friends, they are often talking about spirit beings who are visiting. It seems unfortunate that most parents do not give any credibility to such talk.

Last year I met a new friend, Adrienne, who at the time had lost her husband just a year before. Being Jewish, she was planning the ceremony for the unveiling of her husband's gravestone the next week on the anniversary date. I told her that spirits usually go to their own services and to be on the lookout for a bird or a butterfly that would seem out of place. She mentioned this only to her daughter and no one else. During the ceremony, Adrienne looked over at her daughter who was crying and then she noticed that there was a small bird flying closely around the gravestone. Adrienne is sure that bird was a signal that her husband was keeping an eye on everything.

A few months ago, I was having dinner with Adrienne when she was telling me about her first date since her husband's passing. She had felt having the date would be okay since her daughter had fixed her up with this man. While she was talking, the light above the table suddenly became much brighter. There was obviously a lot of energy around the table, presumably from her husband approving of the date. A few years later, Adrienne got married to this man.

I met Melinda about fifteen years ago in a high tech company. We hit it off almost immediately even though she is almost 20 years younger as we both have engineering backgrounds and we both have a passion for horses, dogs and cats. Also the same as me, Melinda is logical, methodical and down to earth. Ed always liked her a lot. It wasn't until after Ed's passing that I found out about amazing dreams she has every so often. Sometimes she will have premonition dreams like dreaming of a friend's husband being in a bad auto accident; something that actually happened a couple of weeks later. But Melinda does have dreams off and on where she clearly sees and communicates telepathically with deceased pets. Sometimes they are pets who passed a long time ago. Since I believe these dreams to be actual visitations by her pets, I find this comforting evidence that our pets have souls and cross over as well. I have heard and read about pets from a number of sources and believe it to be true. I myself have had only a few dreams with deceased dogs and once my horse, Fleet, who I had from birth to his death 22 years later. Obviously, Fleet and I were very close.

About a year ago, Melinda was diagnosed with colon cancer which she has since successfully fought. But she has told me that, shortly after hearing the diagnosis when she was depressed and in shock, Ed appeared in one of her dreams. She said that he did not say anything but she felt very comforted by his presence.

Wendy is an old friend who I have known for over twenty years. She has told me a number of times about seeing apparitions of her grandparents on different nights in her apartment a number of years ago. They just appeared for a bit and did not say anything. She does describe them as looking a lot younger than they were when they passed. Before Ed passed away, he always considered this pure nonsense and questioned Wendy's sanity. Now I am sure he thinks differently.

Interestingly, the book, *Hello from Heaven*, says that spirits often do look younger when they appear as apparitions.

Wendy also had a remarkable experience while her father was having a liver transplant. She was in the waiting room with the rest of the family when all of a sudden she had the feeling that his mother was there to take him away. She remembers emphatically thinking "Stay away, you cannot have him yet." Later, she found out from the surgeon that there was a time during the operation when they thought they were going to lose her father. Wendy correlated the timeframes to be approximately the same. She never did tell her father about this happening, but he had a story of having seen the Virgin Mary while he was unconscious.

One time while I still had the boat for ocean cruising, I had a friend ask if I could take her and her brother and their spouses in the boat to distribute her parents' ashes. We went about a mile or two beyond the Isle of Shoals, which are a chain of islands six miles off the New Hampshire coast. I headed into the wind and went slowly while they distributed both parents from the stern of the boat. When we went by the islands on the way out, we noticed that a butterfly started following us a few feet from the stern. After distributing the ashes, we took the boat into an island cove where we anchored and had lunch. The butterfly followed us the whole time. We were all convinced that the butterfly was a signal sent by my friend's parents.

I have talked with numerous friends and acquaintances who have been with dying people and have witnessed them seeing and talking with deceased friends or relatives. Numerous books say this is common since the deceased friends and relatives come to help with the transition to the other side. Even though I have not experienced this, I believe it to be true.

CHAPTER SIX

Dreams & Happenings

In Chapter Four, I described a number of the initial signals and happenings that lead me to become a believer. It was almost as though Ed had been trying hard to get my attention by essentially hitting me on the side of the head. Since neither of us had believed in life after death, I am sure when he did pass he was totally shocked to be still alive and would have wanted to tell me. I never did see Ed as an apparition as some of my friends have reported of their husbands, but initially, I really don't know what my reaction would have been if I had seen him appear. I know I would have been shocked, but I don't think I would have been scared considering our bond of love. I have read that, since the spirit world is based on love and compassion, deceased loved ones will not do anything that they believe will shock or upset you. Ed probably knew that I was not ready to see him as an apparition.

Since Ed's passing, I have continued to experience dreams and happenings which reinforce the idea that Ed has been truly around watching after me. Some of the events have been amusing examples of Ed's humor, some have been helpful in making decisions and some have provided comfort when needed. Some events have been more meaningful when considered in combination with other messages. I have logged these events over the last few years to allow me to portray them as accurately as possible. None of these events are made up.

From my research and from my experiences, I believe that dreams that are very distinct and memorable are actual visitations. In the first few months while Ed was trying to get my attention, there were several such dreams with actions or information that would have been unique to Ed.

A month after Ed passed, he came in a dream and told me that he felt great since his chest pains were gone.

A few weeks later, I dreamed that Ed and I were in a crowd of people. He was getting everyone's attention by doing a stunt he used to do in the first few years of our marriage when he had a little too much to drink. He smoked a cigarette down to a third and began flipping it, still burning, in and out of his mouth with his lips without burning himself. Until this dream, I had not thought of this stunt for years. It was distinctly Ed, letting me know he was with me.

A couple of months after that dream, I dreamed that I heard Ed going into the bathroom as I frequently had at night when he was alive. I followed him into the bathroom and saw him vividly. And he said that he loved me. This was all a dream but it left me feeling warm and loved every time I thought about it for days later.

One amusing chain of events began during that first summer. We had been subscribing to DirecTV for our television reception for several years. Ed had mounted the satellite dish on the railing of the front deck where we could easily reach it to remove snow. As folks who have a satellite dish know, the reception is frequently interrupted when there is a bad rain or snow storm. A message will come on the TV screen saying "Searching for Signal." When Ed was alive, he was known for playing tricks on friends by putting his hand in front of the dish receiver to interrupt the signal. The "Searching for Signal" message seemed to interrupt my television viewing a lot in the months following Ed's passing. Knowing how Ed could fool around, I began blaming it on him. In October shortly after becoming a believer, I had a dream where Ed came and told me that the satellite dish was no good and he should throw it away. I pleaded for him to leave it there. The dream was so real that I had to check the railing of the deck when I got up to make sure it was still there, and I was relieved to see it was. However a few days later, the TV reception went to the "Searching for Signal" message and it did not come back. I called DirecTV customer support and, after having me try several things to fix it, they decided they would send a repairman to take a look. When the repairman got there, the first thing he said was "This satellite dish is no good. I will have to install a new one." I was close to telling him that my dead husband had told me that last week, but I didn't. Replacing the dish did fix the problem.

In August when I distributed Ed's ashes at the lake, we used the boats of three couples of friends to get us to the cove for the ceremony. One of the couples told me a few months later, that their outboard motor had not worked well before that day and did not work again after that day. But that day, it worked perfectly. I don't know how it happened, but I am glad it worked well to get Ed's ashes to the designated location.

In October, I took a friend with me to the cabin in Maine the weekend that I was going to be draining the pipes and shutting down for the winter for the first time by myself. When we were unloading Ed's Chevy Tahoe, both in Maine Friday night and at home the end of the weekend, we heard a funny pinging noise like a thin metal gas can popping out. The noise came from the Tahoe both times. I believe that Ed was telling me he was there to help. At various times after that, I heard that sound when I had the

Tahoe. Now I have different car but I will frequently hear that type of sound when I am working in my garage. I have never found the source of the noise, but I suspect somehow Ed is causing it.

That same weekend when I was in Maine shutting down for the first time, my friend, Beth, called me to check on things. When I told her that nothing much had been happening, we immediately got disconnected. Beth called back and said "So nothing much has happened?" She was sure that Ed had caused the phone issue.

Also that same weekend in October, some old friends who lived two cabins away told me that they were having funny things happen. Their toilet would not stop running and a heater in their living room would turn off by itself. These were the same friends that Ed once told "If you are right and there is life after death and if something happens to me, then I will come back and watch you in the bathroom!"

A month later one day when I went out to my barn, I realized that the light bulb in one of the stalls that had been burned out for a year was now fixed. I had not changed it and no one else was around who would have done it either.

The clock in the garage near Ed's workbench, which would sometimes tick loudly and sometimes not at all, often was a reliable indicator of Ed's presence and therefore gave me a lot of comfort. The next year when I moved to my new condo, I made sure to move that clock and immediately mount it in my new garage on the wall above the workbench. After moving, it continued to act sporadically for about another year and a half until I assumed that the battery had finally died. It was stopped on one time for several months. Until one day when I was feeling depressed, I was surprised to see it running again, but then I realized that Ed probably had given it a jolt of energy to let me know he was with me and to cheer me up. It ran for two or three more days before stopping again. I have left it on the wall, stopped on one time. I know that someday it will start again when Ed has a message for me.

The last few years of his life when he first got up, Ed loved watching *Imus in the Morning* and listening to the interviews while he drank his morning coffee. I found Imus a little tedious. So once Ed was gone, I began watching the Fox News Channel. I got in the habit of coming downstairs in the morning, turning on Fox and going into the kitchen to start coffee. However one morning, I was in the kitchen and realized that I was hearing Imus and not Fox. I went in the living room to double check the TV. And it was the channel for Imus instead of the Fox News Channel which I know I had turned on. I left it on Imus for a while and was surprised about 15 minutes later when Imus had an interview with Laura Ingraham. Ed loved Laura Ingraham since he had followed her career from when she was in college and began writing for the Dartmouth College newspaper which he subscribed to.

I truly believe that Ed wanted to listen to this interview himself and changed the channel. I have had similar events happen since then that confirm this belief. A few months ago, I was driving in the car when the radio (which was turned off) came on to Rush Limbaugh on the talk radio station where I had left the radio. Rush was talking about Bill Clinton and whether or not Clinton had passed up chances to get Osama bin Laden. This was a subject that had interested Ed tremendously when he was alive, since he had read a book by a retired Secret Service agent who wrote about missed chances to get Osama bin Laden due to Clinton. I know that Ed wanted to listen when he turn on my car radio.

There have been a number of times when Ed has turned on the car radio, however not always to listen himself. Some of the time, I believe that he just wants to let me know he is there for my support. Once about a year ago, I was driving to an appointment with a new doctor and was listening to the *Imus in the Morning* show. As I got closer to the doctor's office, I was in traffic and I turned off the radio so I could concentrate. A few minutes later as I pulled into the parking lot, the radio came back on again. I think Ed was saying that he would be with me for the appointment.

Ed always loved it when I would do challenging things not often done by women. When I finally bought a new outboard motor for the small, aluminum boat in Maine, I began launching, running and putting the boat in the garage by myself. As I pulled the car away from the garage after my first solo boating adventure, the car radio came on. I know Ed was telling me that I was doing a good job and he was proud of me.

It is always great to know that I am never really alone.

One time on a very cold, icy night, I met a friend for dinner. When I got back in the car and started home after dinner, I realized that the car was in 4 wheel drive, but I know that I had not put it in 4 wheel drive before dinner. Ed wanted to make sure I got home safely.

I have also had a number of times when the dials for the seat heaters have been turned on. I know these are all ways of letting me know he is with me giving me his love.

I have suspected a number of times that Ed enjoys being with me when I am going somewhere or doing something that he wants to experience as well. One time a few weeks after moving into my new house, I had hired my captain friend, Phil, to go out with me on the big boat that Ed loved. Phil and I got into a conversation about what we watch on TV. I commented that I end up turning on the Fox News Channel most of the time. I admitted that I was a bit tired of it but it was habit. The next morning I got up and started to turn on Fox News. But something got mixed up and I went instead to the Country Music station. Since this was a new cable TV provider for me, I did not even know where this station was. I am sure that Ed was with me on the boat listening to me and interfered with my channel selection to show me there are other channels to listen to.

As I described in an earlier chapter, in the first six months or so after Ed passed, I would get short, quick muscle spasms or Charlie horses in my legs which I soon identified as being signals from Ed's energy around me. But through the first winter, these stopped and I began to be aware once in a while of very slight muscle twitches in my legs. Since I had never had twitches like this before and since I was not getting any more Charlie horses, I believed that Ed's energy was becoming more subtle with his signals. Then the next fall, the slight muscle twitches stopped happening and seemed to be replaced with waves of goose bumps that happened only on my legs. Again since I cannot remember ever having had goose bumps on my legs before, I am convinced that they are signals from Ed. Whenever I feel the goose bumps, I think thoughts of love and appreciation and thank Ed for being with me. Even though I have come to know that he does know what I am thinking, I sometimes give him a "thumbs up" signal.

The waves of goose bumps still happen to me although they are not quite as frequent as they were initially. They can happen when I am having dinner with a friend, when I am listening to music, when I am watching television and during other activities. I can usually realize a reason why

I am getting a signal, such as familiar music or a familiar television show. Sometimes though, the subject is not familiar but has something to do with love, death or the spirit world. I have had cases when the car radio is just beginning a song which I have never heard before. When I listen to the words, I realize why Ed would have been giving me a signal about that particular song. I have tried hard to objectively analyze when these goose bumps happen and whether or not I am causing them. I have concluded that I cannot control or generate these goose bumps. And sometimes when I think they will happen, they don't, making me believe that Ed is not always with me.

There have been times when I have gotten other evidence that the goose bumps are from Ed. Once was when I met my friend, Melinda, for lunch at a very nice, New England country inn. Melinda is the one who I mentioned in the last chapter who has had dreams communicating with deceased pets and who had a comforting dream where Ed visited her shortly after she was diagnosed with cancer. This particular lunch was a few months after that dream. I had not seen Melinda since well before her cancer diagnosis. Off and on through the time we were together, I got goose bumps which I believe was Ed saying he was there as well. Without mentioning it to Melinda, on the way home I stopped at a shopping center and bought a new VCR/DVD player to install on my primary TV.

The next week when I called Melinda, she told me that night after meeting for lunch she had focused on Ed before she went to sleep. She had asked that he give her some messages in her dreams that she could tell me. She said that she got two different things that meant nothing to her but she thought she would tell me. The first was that Ed told her he was looking forward to watching movies with me. Melinda had not known about the new VCR/DVD player. And the second thing Melinda got from Ed was just the image of the roof of a salt box house. Salt box houses are distinctly an old New England architecture. I believe that Ed used the salt box roof to let Melinda know that he was with us at lunch at the old country inn. For me, these messages were confirmation of the goose bumps that I felt during lunch were from Ed. I also want to note that Melinda is not a medium or psychic. She was originally a software engineer and now is in software management in a computer company.

In the first year after Ed's passing, I found that there were several instances of my receiving signals which proved out not to be from Ed.

The first fall when I was getting the short muscle spasms in my lower legs which I believe were from Ed, I also began getting periodic muscle twitches in my right forearm when I was in bed lying on my right side with my arm up. Of course, I assumed they were from Ed and was pleased as I could talk to him and sometimes get them to happen on request. However in December when I went for the first time to a medium, April, I asked what kind of signals Ed was giving me. When April had no answer right away, I asked if there were any signals having to do with my arm. At that April immediately came back with the answer that was my father and not Ed. April also picked up on the family strife that happened before my father passed. She said that my father was trying to make amends for the family conflict. I was shocked that my father would send signals allowing me to think they were from Ed. I have since forgiven my father for all the awful things he had said and had done to me before his passing, but at the time, I was still very upset with him. When I got home, I announced into the air hoping to influence the spirits that I only wanted to hear from Ed and no one else. Those muscle twitches on my right arm have never happened again.

Another time one November evening, I was sitting in my living room alone talking to Ed when the phone rang just once several times. When I answered on my portable phone, the phone was just dead and had no noise. I have since read that spirits have been known to try to communicate by using the phone this way, but sometimes people will actually hear the voice of their loved one. However, I did not get a voice. Then several different times, I had the portable phone ring by itself without any wall phone in the house ringing. Once after hanging up, I noticed that the light on the two line kitchen wall phone was still on for the primary line. I went into the kitchen and picked that phone up and it was also dead. I hung up and saw that the light was still on. I watched as it flickered off slowly. This series of events with the phone did bother me as it was so weird, but I assumed it was further communications with Ed.

Over the course of the next couple of weeks, I had similar occurrences with the phone including one Sunday afternoon when an old friend, Bill, was helping me cut up firewood on the farm. When we came in for lunch, the phone began ringing just once and was dead when I answered it. I thought to myself that Ed was not happy with the way Bill was using his chain saw and wood splitter. At first Bill said that he thought that the phone company must be working on the lines even though it was Sunday. When the phone continued to act like this, Bill asked if it happened often. I did not want to tell him what I thought it was.

One night shortly after that Sunday, I was feeling lonely and began asking Ed to make the phone act like that again so I would know he was there. Later that night, Ed came to me in a dream and told me not to wish for the phone to act that way as it would probably be other spirits. I have not asked for that kind of signal again. And it has not happened again. I believe that Ed will always be my guardian angel looking out for me.

During that first winter, an old Navy friend, Al, called me to see how I was doing. He and Ed had been in the same squadron together and had kept in occasional contact through the years. In the course of the conversation, I told him that I had found a file Ed had kept with information from the Internet about their squadron and some of the pilots who had been shot down in Vietnam. Then I mentioned that Ed is probably with some of them now. Of course, while I was on that subject, I could not resist talking about some of my experiences. I told him about the episodes of beeping when I was on the phone talking about selling the big boat and getting out of boating. A couple of minutes later in our conversation, the phone beeped twice a minute apart. Al heard the beeps as well and commented that it sounded like I have call answering. I told him that I did not have call answering and that it was probably Ed listening in. I don't think I convinced Al since shortly afterwards he ended the conversation saying that he and his wife would call to get together. They never did. I think that Ed intentionally wanted to get a rise out of Al. I always have a good chuckle whenever I think of that phone call.

There have been times when I have had dreams that confirm that Ed is very aware of major events in my life. In June of 2004, two months before moving into my newly constructed condo, I had several dreams that demonstrate this.

On June 11th, I received delivery of a big dumpster to allow me to clean out the two garages more quickly. That night I dreamed that Ed came in a distinct dream and said that he would help me cleaning out things.

One week later, I dreamed that Ed came and said that he would oversee the construction of the new condo for me.

And one week after that, I dreamed that we were together enjoying boating on the lake in Maine. I asked Ed if he wanted to go over and see our new condo area after boating. He said definitely. I then realized that it would be a surprise for me to walk into the model home and introduce Ed to the realtor who I knew quite well.

The next May, I had plans to move the big boat to a new marina in Gloucester, MA. A few days before the move, I had a dream where Ed came and told me that he would be boating with me. Since I had been anxious about coordinating the move, I found this dream comforting.

And other times I have had dreams in combination with various signals which give me support and advice for getting through problems. As I have mentioned before, when Ed passed away I was working in a high pressure, high tech job. For the several years, I had been the "Release Manager" in a software organization which supported online services which had to be available 24/7. It was my job to oversee and coordinate all the enhancements and fixes going into production in monthly releases. I had to insure that every change was properly tested and all dependencies were considered. I loved the job as it required a lot of attention to detail which is one of my strengths. However about a year and a half after Ed's passing, I found the job increasingly stressful as the whole environment became totally chaotic after many reorganizations. It was harder and harder to insure quality releases into production. Then I was reorganized to work for a jerk. I went through several months of complete frustration and finally decided to take early retirement. But throughout these months, I got support and confidence from signals and messages from Ed.

I mentioned in the last chapter, since Ed and I met in a chemistry lab, Ed would create the scent of a solvent like acetone to let me know he was there. I began smelling acetone a number of times during those months. It usually happened at particularly stressful times while I was driving to work.

One time after a hard day at work, I came out to my car and opened the back door to put my canvas bag on the back seat. On the back seat floor, I saw a small, metal, silver colored star which I had never seen before and had no idea where it could have come from. Then when I got a mile or so from home, I began smelling acetone. Considering these two things together, I believe that Ed put the little star there to give me confidence. I still have the little star and I keep it with other items from Ed.

In February of 2005 in a reading with Pat, the gifted medium who I will talk about more in the next chapter, I asked what I should do about work. Through Pat, Ed told me to trust my instincts. (It is normal for the spirit world not to tell you exactly what to do as they do not want to interfere with your free will.)

The next month, I oversaw a huge, highly visible software release into production, and then the next day I had to address a lot of issues resulting from the release. The night in between these two stressful days, I had the only dream I have had about Grizz, the big Australian Shepherd that died a few months before Ed. When Grizz was alive, he would only go in swimming on his own terms. He hated getting into water when we wanted. We would have to pull him in against his will. In my dream that night, I was in a swimming pool and had to get Grizz into the water. This time, Grizz jumped willingly into my arms and telepathically told me that I have to trust my instincts as he trusted me.

After having had the same message from Ed the month before, I realized that I needed to go with my gut feeling and retire early to get away from the stress and insanity in that work environment. I laugh when I think about having told a few people that Grizz, my old dead dog, told me to take early retirement. Although that was stretching the truth a little, Grizz' message did have a profound effect.

Even though I had made up my mind to retire, I waited until the end of June to have an additional year of employment to be counted toward retirement. In the meantime, I had two amazing dreams which, when considered together, really helped my confidence. In the end of May in the first dream, Ed came and told me telepathically that he would always be behind me with everything I do in life. For some reason in this dream, he looked much younger than he had when he passed away. The second dream came about two weeks later when I was at the cabin in Maine. In the early morning, I dreamed that Ed got into bed with me and put his arm around me. And then he said "You are going first." Assuming that he was talking about death, I responded to him "But you went first." At that Ed's answer was "That depends which way you look at it." It was not until later in the morning after waking up that I remembered the dream from two weeks earlier. Then it made perfect sense that my going first matched with Ed always being behind me. To me, these are some of the best dreams I have had. I feel great whenever I think of them.

In the last chapter, I talked about how people will often have signs such as birds or butterflies appear which confirm the presence of their loved ones. I don't understand how this happens. I wonder whether a bird or butterfly is sent by the spirit world or if the spirit takes on that particular form to send the signal. Maybe I should not question this, but the scientist in me wants to understand. One book I read was by a man who could will himself to have out of body experiences. In the book he detailed what it was like and how he documented the experiences from a scientific perspective. At one point, he said that when he was out of his body, he could take on the look of anything he wanted just by focusing his thoughts. Again, I don't know or understand how these signs happen, but this is the most feasible explanation I have seen. I do know that there is currently a lot of scientific investigation into how powerful thoughts are. Without an exact explanation, I have had at least several times seeing birds which I know were signals from Ed.

At the lake in Maine, Ed and I were always on the lookout for a Bald Eagle and valued every sighting. Ed was much better at spotting them that I was. We did not see them often but would usually see them several times a year. A year after Ed's passing, I was sitting on our dock as Ed and I had loved to do. All of a sudden, I looked up and saw a Bald Eagle about a quarter mile away from me flying directly toward me at twenty feet above the water. He continued to fly directly at me until he was almost over me and then he swerved to fly down the waterfront for a ways before flying inland and disappearing. To me this was way more than a coincidence.

A few weeks later, when I arrived at the cabin for a weekend, I went down to the waterfront to look at the lake as I usually do. I immediately saw a Bald Eagle flying around a little away from me. When he landed in a tree about 600' from me, I waited a minute and then said softly "Okay, Ed have him fly now." And the Eagle flew. This may have been coincidence, but I don't think so.

A few months after selling the horse farm, I went back for a visit with the new owners. Of course, visiting the farm that Ed and I built would be an event that would have interested him. The new owners are also spiritual and are familiar with possible spiritual signals like the appearance of birds. The wife, Kay, and I were standing near the horse barn looking up toward the riding ring which was more than 100 feet away. Kay saw some crows in the ring and said "Oh, there's Ed!" I told then her that I did not think that would be Ed since there are a lot of crows around. After talking for a few more minutes, we both looked up and saw a crow flying toward us at 8 to 10 feet in the air. We watched as the crow flew directly over me. He was so close that we could hear the whoosh sound of his wings going through the air. It also seemed that the bird had appeared out of nowhere. Again, I am convinced that this was not a coincidence. It was Ed!

The first winter in my new condo, I spent a lot of time decorating with both new furniture and new framed pictures. In my bedroom and my office, I decided to have framed pictures from some of the best times with Ed and the pets. One Sunday morning, I was going through old photos to determine which ones should be enlarged and which ones should be used in a frame with a collage matte. As usual when reviewing old photos, it became a very emotional time with all the memories of old times. I had put the frame with the collage matte flat on a table to more easily plan which photos were to go where. I had all but one of the matte openings planned leaving a section with just the glass of the frame underneath when I had to stop to take the dogs for a walk. When I got back and looked at the open section in between all the pictures, I realized that there was a waxy, greasy substance on the glass that had not been there before. While I do not know what this substance was or how it got there, I have a strong feeling that it was due to a strong emotional reaction from Ed. It makes sense to me that we were both greatly saddened by reviewing our lives in photos. Mediums in books I have read say that a spirit who has crossed over retains the same personality. I am sure that Ed and I would have had the same reaction to the photos.

When I was working, I kept two cars, one of them being a Honda for commuting. A month after retiring, I decided that I really should sell the Honda since I no longer needed to maintain it. Instead of trying to advertise and sell it myself, I wanted to see what a particular used car dealer would offer me for it. So I headed out to run some errands and get the car washed before stopping by the used car dealer. At the first stop at the drug store, I realized that my cash consisted of small change, $12 in bills and a $100 bill. Luckily, the $12 covered the cash I needed for the drug store and the car wash. After having been in and out of the car all afternoon doing errands and stopping at the used car dealer, I decided to stop at a farm stand for fresh vegetables for dinner. As I drove up to the stand, I thought to myself how weird that all I had was some small change and a $100 bill and that I had better make sure not to buy more than I could pay for with the change I had. Having bought the vegetables, I got back in the car and immediately saw a $10 bill laid flat on the driver's side floor. I know that I did not have a $10 bill in the car. I also know that nothing had been on the car floor as I had been in and out of the car all afternoon and I had been trying to keep the car clean. My only explanation is that Ed wanted me to have something more than the one large $100 bill in case of an emergency.

I have kept that ten dollar bill along with the small metal star and other unexplainable things from Ed in a glass top coffee table. The other things include Ed's guitar pick which showed up on the basement floor of my new condo, two almonds in their shells which showed up in an open box in my new garage and a few pieces of potpourri which came out of a vase and were lying on the table one morning. I also have kept Ed's watch which had worked until the battery went dead a couple of years after his passing. When I found the watch had stopped, I realized that it stopped with the day of the week blank and the date of the month at 26. Ed's birthday was September 26th. I do not understand it, but I think that was no coincidence.

These are some of the more remarkable experiences I have had which make me know that Ed is truly with me. I have had many more but these are the ones that I can decisively say were caused by or were from Ed. As I said in the beginning, I have not made any of them up and I have tried to be accurate in my portrayals. Some people will probably say that some of them are coincidences or my imagination. But it would be hard to say that they are all figments of my imagination. I know that I am not the only person to have had such experiences. Many other people have had similar things happen with their loved ones.

It is always very comforting to know that your relationship with your loved one lives on. Be sure to look for the little things happening around you and be sure not to rationalize them away. Your loved one is probably trying to say "I'm here and I still love you." Be open to possible communications.

CHAPTER SEVEN

Mediums & Intuitive Friends

Who would go to a medium? Mediums and psychics are people who make money by playing on the emotions of sad, grieving people, usually little old ladies. That's what I used to believe. Sure, there were times when I went with friends to a palm reader or a tarot card reader, but that was just for the fun of it. I never took them seriously. I thought that they were on the fringe of society and only weak people would be sucked into spending more than fun money with them.

But after having experienced several months of signals from Ed and finally accepting that Ed was with me in spirit, I realized that there is life after death and I needed to be open to new ways of thinking. The first books I read were by James Van Praagh, a medium known around the world. His book, *Talking to Heaven*, began with how he realized he had paranormal abilities when he was young and then went into descriptions of how mediums and psychics receive messages. Since I found these explanations helpful to my understanding of how medium communications work, I thought that the following excerpt from *Talking to Heaven* would be the best way to help your understanding.

Those who are able to tune into the faster vibration of the spirit body after death, either in a physical or a mental way, are called *sensitives* or *mediums*. As the term suggests, a medium is an individual who is a middleman or mediator, a person who goes between the spiritual and physical worlds. A medium is able to use energy to reach through the thin veil separating the physical life from the spiritual life. A way of looking at the concept of mediumship is as follows: Human beings are made of the superconscious, the subconscious, and the conscious minds. In mediumship all thoughts, feelings, and sights are transmitted through a medium's superconscious, or spirit mind. We all are constantly picking up spirit impressions in this way, but it is the medium who is able to interpret them. The message then moves into the conscious mind and is revealed.

The term "psychic" is often used as a catchall phrase for anyone who works in the paranormal. Everyone is psychic to some degree or another, but not everyone is a medium. A medium is *not* a fortune teller. In other words, mediums are psychic, but not all psychics are mediums. Psychism and mediumship use the same mechanics of the mind, but mediumship differs from "being psychic," or psychism. Like mediumship, psychism is telepathic. Telepathy is another word for mind-to-mind communication. For example, you are with a friend, and you say exactly what he is thinking. Your friend responds by saying, "You must be psychic." A person who is psychic is able to read an inanimate object or a person by tuning into the energy that emanates from the object or person. It is in this aura of the object or person that a psychic interprets revelations of the past and the future of the item or person. A psychic may also receive the energy of the object or person by feeling or seeing. Because there is no time in the energy world, few psychics can give an accurate time frame about the information received.

On the other hand, a medium, or sensitive, is a person who is able to feel and/or hear thoughts, voices, or mental impressions from the spirit world. Spirits also use telepathy. A medium is able to become completely receptive to the higher frequencies or energies on which spirit people vibrate. Hence, the mind of a spirit melds or impresses itself on the superconscious mind of a medium. From there, the message goes into the conscious mind, and a medium reveals what a spirit is thinking or feeling. Mediumship is much more involved than basic psychism because a medium is opening him/herself to a discarnate energy. In psychism, the information does not come from a discarnate spirit who resides on a higher frequency level. A discarnate uses much of a medium's life energy to send its message. A medium works directly with a spirit, and the two have to be willing to take part in the communication process; otherwise there is no communication.

The concept of mediumship is more easily apparent in dreams. Many times we dream of relatives or friends who have passed over. The dream feels so real that we swear we were indeed with them. We feel strongly about it. This is because while in our dream state we were actually with our loved ones on a spiritual plane. When we sleep, our etheric or astral body travels in nonearthly realms where we encounter our loved ones and are able to communicate with them.

Mediumship itself can be broken down into two distinct categories. The first and most common type is mental mediumship. As the word mental denotes, the form of mediumship utilizes the mind – the intuitive or cosmic mind, not the rational or logical part. This type of mental mediumship falls into several distinct types: clairvoyance, clairaudience, clairsentience, and inspirational thought.

Clairvoyance

Derived from the French language, *clairvoyance* means "clear vision." A clairvoyant applies her innate sense of inner sight to see objects, colors, symbols, people, spirits, or scenes. These pictures are not visible to the naked eye and usually flash into the medium's mind as if she were physically seeing.

In most cases the sights should be recognizable to the person for whom she is reading, whom I refer to as the sitter.

Clairaudience

This term means "clear hearing." A Clairaudient hears with the psychic ear or sensitized ear. He is able to hear sounds, names, voices, and music that vibrate on a higher frequency. Much like dogs that hear at a higher frequency range than humans, mediums, too, hear beyond our normal hearing range. A clairaudient provides the sitter exactly what he hears from the higher rate of vibration. Although he hears the actual spirit voices or whispers with the same inflection the person would have used on the earth, he tells the sitter in his own voice what he is hearing.

Clairsentience

This is a form of mental mediumship that means "clear feeling." A medium with clairsentience is able to sense when spirits are in the room. A true clairsentient will usually feel the *spirit personality* coming through his entire being. He is able to give messages to the sitter by way of strong, empathetic feelings and emotions from the spirit. In clairsentience, not only is the mind of a medium used but a medium's emotional body as well.

Inspirational Thought

This is also known as inspirational speaking, inspirational writing, or inspirational art. In inspirational thought, a medium receives thoughts, impressions, knowledge – all without forethought. It differs from clairsentience because the emotional state is *not* as evident in inspirational thought as it is with a *spirit personality* coming through to speak. Inspirational thought is very objective. It has neither the intense emotions nor the spirit personality attached to the message. These are associated with clairsentience. Although inspirational thought comes from spirit, the personality of a spirit is not impressed on the receiver.

Now I understood conceptually how mediums were supposed to work, but I was still hesitant. I really did not consider going to a medium to be the way for me, but at the same time, I was curious. As I wrote earlier, when I joined a bereavement group formed to help people through the holiday season, I immediately became friends with Anna who had also lost her husband suddenly. She told me how she had been to a local medium for a couple of fantastic readings. This intrigued me further, but not enough to make an appointment for myself.

At Thanksgiving, I spent the weekend in Connecticut with my friend, Bea and her husband. Because we were going to be away for the day of Thanksgiving, Bea hired her dog sitter, Nancy, to walk the dogs. Bea described Nancy as being psychic. To get a further conversation going I asked what she meant by that, Bea told me that Nancy was very psychic in many ways and could feel their house was full of spirits with one being Bea's father. She also said that she had even seen her father once herself.

When we returned later that evening, Nancy had left me a nice note and a book, *Journey of Souls* by Michael Newton. I have kept her note and still find it heart warming to read:

With warmest thought: Your husband [who is <u>very much</u> alive and well] gets to <u>listen</u> to your deepest self – the parts that were "unfinished" when he died. Listening, I think, is very powerful for the soul; so the two of you continue to communicate and grow far beyond "death"!

Always Love, Nancy
p.s. He can talk back in dreams.

For a long time, every time I read Nancy's note, I broke down into tears. It was great to get confirmation from someone else that Ed was with me. Later when I read *Journey of Souls,* I found it to be a fascinating and thought provoking book. It was by a Psychologist who has hypnotized people to have them access memories in their superconscious minds and describe what life is like in the spirit world before birth.

The next day I talked with Nancy on the phone to thank her. She offered to do a tarot card reading for me and agreed on a time for us to get together to review her findings. It was all fascinating but strange at the same time. The results of Nancy's tarot card reading were not completely accurate, but there was enough truth to be an exciting experience. I decided that when I got home I would make an appointment with the medium Anna had been to. I knew that I could judge for myself what was accurate, and I wanted to try it.

I went to April twice in the month of December. April's building was a strange place and it made me hope no one I knew would see me enter. The sign out front was weird and the entrance was full of psychic stuff for sale. She tape recorded each session so that I could have a copy at the end. That was nice except that the second time I went the tape was blank when I got home. I have since heard that very often electronic things do not work right if there are strong spirits around. I had mixed feelings about April. I don't think she was faking anything, and I do think that she was working to the best of her ability. In the end, I estimate that she was maybe only 40-45% accurate for me. Some things were good, but others were way out in left field.

April did pick up on the strife and conflicts that had happened in my family in the previous few years. And she did say that my father was very unhappy with the last years of his life and he was trying to make amends with me. I believe this to be true since my father's attitude toward me had changed tremendously from his younger years when we had a good relationship. In his old age, he had been manipulated by my younger brother and his wife for their own gain. They had managed to turn both my parents against Ed and me by playing on their elderly paranoia. So April's portrayal of my father was no surprise.

Another thing that April told me was that in two to three years I would have a career change. At the time, I thought this was ridiculous as I liked my job, it paid well and had great benefits. I had no idea that in a year and a half I would be retiring and trying my luck at writing this book.

Another surprising but rather amusing thing that April said at the end of the first reading was "Who is Bernadette?" Since Bernadette is an unusual name, it seems like no coincidence that my older brother's wife is Bernadette. I told April that was my brother's wife, and that she was still alive. April said "But her father isn't, is he?" I replied that he had died a long time ago, over twenty-five years ago. April then said that he was there and wanted to get the message to Bernadette that she would be all right. I really did not know what this referred to, but I thought that I should tell my brother, Brien, what happened and relay the message.

When I called to tell Brien this message, I got a cool reception. Brien, a Born Again Christian, informed me that the Bible says that you are not supposed to talk with the dead so he really did not want the news. But after talking a few minutes, my brother in a very logical fashion said, "I guess if the Bible says that you are not supposed to talk with the dead, it means that it IS possible to talk to the dead." He then said that he would give the message to Bernadette.

A few months later in another conversation with Brien, he told me that message was exactly the type of thing that Bernadette's father would have said. I believe that spirits who have not been able to communicate will use remote relationships like this to communicate a message.

A few weeks later, the end of January, James Van Praagh was on the Larry King Show for an hour of live readings for viewer call-ins. I began calling the 800 number published on the screen as soon as it was put up in hopes of having a reading. But since the line seemed to be hopelessly busy, I gave up so I could concentrate on watching the show. About halfway through the show, there was a call which was obviously a total mismatch between the caller and the messages from James. But the messages completely matched my situation with Ed.

Here is the CNN transcript for that part of the show with my comments in bold:

CALLER: Hello, James?

VAN PRAAGH: Yes, dear.

CALLER: It's a privilege to talk to you.

VAN PRAAGH: Thank you.

CALLER: I lost my husband…

VAN PRAAGH: I know. He's right…

CALLER: … in 2001.

VAN PRAAGH: ... next to you. He's right next to you, sweetheart.

CALLER: Is he?

VAN PRAAGH: Let me just tell you something. You've been writing a letter to him after he died or there's talk about writing, OK? And he was writing before he died? [**Ed had written and published his own Western novel and had several books underway when he died.**]

CALLER: No. Not that I know of.

VAN PRAAGH: OK. Who was writing something? Did you write something about him?

CALLER: We wrote a beautiful eulogy that...

VAN PRAAGH: OK. I don't know if that's it. I want to talk about writing something about him, so I don't know if it's a biography about him or someone's still joking about doing that. [**I am writing this book about Ed right now.**]

CALLER: I don't...

VAN PRAAGH: OK. Hold on. Hold on. What's his first name?

CALLER: Joseph.

VAN PRAAGH: Joseph?

CALLER: Or Joe.

VAN PRAAGH: OK. Is there an Ed somewhere, someone named Ed or Eddie? [**I usually called him Ed, but I sometimes used Eddie to tease him as that is what his mother called him.**] *Because I want to keep it if you don't, because I get that.*

CALLER: No, I don't know of an Ed.

VAN PRAAGH: Also, I want to ask you, is there a chair you're sitting next to you that's empty right now?

CALLER: A chair next to me that's empty?

VAN PRAAGH: That's empty.

CALLER: No, I'm sitting in a chair that he always sat in.

VAN PRAAGH: OK. He's talking about sitting in an empty chair, so whatever that means. [**As I wrote earlier, I always suspected that Ed would sit in the empty chair next to his office desk when I was doing something critical on his computer.**] *There's a chair across from you. There's something right across from the chair he's talking to me about.* [**Ed's desk was across from the chair.**]

CALLER: There's a chair across from me.

VAN PRAAGH: Hello, OK. And there's also a clock right near there on the wall, OK? And he's talking about a clock not working. [**This has got to refer to the broken clock in the garage that Ed used to get my attention**

shortly after he passed.] *So I want to pay attention to that, OK? I also want to tell you, did you hear him speak to you when you were sleeping?* [**Ed has frequently spoken to me in my dreams. I talked about these communications in earlier chapters.**]

CALLER: No.

VAN PRAAGH: OK.

CALLER: I never have.

At this point, Larry King realizing the extent of the mismatch interrupted with talk that his father's name was Ed and he could have been there. James Van Praagh replied that he could have.

I was and I am sure that this was my Ed sending me messages. When Ed was alive, we frequently watched the Larry King Show in the evening. He would have been amused by being on that show.

A few weeks later, when I was on the phone with Beth talking about ways that Ed's appearance on the Larry King Show might have been possible, we both experienced having our voices suddenly sound very distant as though we were a million miles apart. It was one of the weirdest things, but it seemed like the conversation had evoked some kind of strange energy or reaction.

After the Larry King Show and after having read several James Van Praagh books, I decided to see if I could get a reading with James. At his website, I learned that he no longer gives private readings, but he does have a list of a dozen or so mediums who are supposed to be reputable. I read through the list trying to determine if I would want to employ any of them. They were all pretty far away from my home in New Hampshire. I became interested in the fact that most of them said that they do telephone readings, and I wondered if phone readings could be accurate. I decided that the only way to know would be to try one and judge for myself if they were worthwhile. I picked a woman, Patricia Gagliardo, in Connecticut with the idea that I could drive there if I wanted in the future. But since I was still working, it would not have been easy or practical to make the drive initially.

Just to try it, I contacted Patricia to find out how to pay and schedule a half hour reading. And soon I was having my first amazing phone reading.

When we started, Pat asked me to say something so she could adjust to my voice. I said that I was hoping to communicate with my husband. That was all I said. Other than that, she knew my name. Here is a summary of the highlights from my notes for that half hour with my comments in bold:

- Ed was communicating with her. **Pat always refers to Ed, not by name, but as "the spirit of your husband." I am sure that is the most accurate way of referring to him because, in spirit, he really is not Ed anymore. But I still use Ed.**

- She immediately mentioned, Richard, my younger brother. She said that he does not live in reality and that I should tell him to reprioritize his life to what is important, not the material things. I should tell him this by sending him a card and emphasize the effect on his two daughters. [**I never have sent my brother a card since our relationship is poor after the family conflicts and he would not have appreciated the comments. It is true that he loves his material things as he has always said "Nothing is too good for a good Christian." It is also true that my brother has two daughters. I want to note that I have learned that once someone crosses over, their perspective on life changes to that of love and compassion. These comments from Ed would have been made constructively and not critically.**]

- Pat commented that I have a strong will and have done well through a lot of problems. [**I am sure that this was referring to all the problems with my family, both my parents passing away and Ed's own passing.**]

- Ed always loved pickup trucks and he has one now in the spirit world. [**Ed did love his trucks.**]

- **[At the time of this reading, I was still living in the house we had built but had money down to buy my new house.]** Pat described the house we had built with a large deck and she knew there was a room which was still unfinished. She said that Ed apologized for not having finished the room and he thought that I should have it finished before putting the house up for sale. **[There was space in the upstairs of the attached two car garage which was unfinished. Ed always intended to finish it into a large bedroom with an additional bathroom. Since the house had only two bedrooms, we had discussed many times the fact that the property would be worth a lot more with that as a third bedroom. When Ed passed, it was partially framed in and partially wired.]**

- She said that Ed was glad that I was moving. And she knew that the new house was near a school. **[My new house is near a middle school]**.

- I asked who had met Ed when he crossed over. Pat said that she thought there were two male spirits, one with the initial H and one being William. **[William was Ed's father's name, so it makes sense that his father was there. The**

"H" initial is ambiguous, but information in future readings has given me the impression that the other male was his grandfather on his father's side. I think the "H" is for the family name of "Hewson." There will be more about this later.]

- Pat commented that Ed had been stubborn, but she knew that he was a wonderful man. [**She repeated he was a wonderful man a couple of times. I don't think she was saying it just for my benefit. Of course, I know she was right.**]

- She also described a black and white dog that was with Ed now. [**That must have been Grizz, Ed's big dog.**]

- At the end of the half hour, she said that Ed wants me to live well.

Considering before the reading, Pat only knew my name and the fact that my husband had passed, the information she conveyed was almost unbelievable. I realized at the end of the half hour that there is a night and day difference between just any medium and one as gifted as Pat. I was intrigued with the idea of further communications with Ed and decided that it would be worth spending more money to see what I could find out.

Over the next few months, I launched into having a series of readings with Pat, usually one every week or two. They became an extension of my research into what Ed had gone through as well as a big help in healing my grief. In every reading there was always information from Ed which confirmed that he had been around me recently and knew what I had been doing. This would be done with a description of some new decoration in the house, some new activity I was doing or some phone call I had made. There would often be comments about friends or relatives with their particular problems or health issues. Sometimes I would get warnings or advice about things I should be doing.

I learned that when mediums hear words or phrases, they usually hear only partial syllables so they have to interpret the overall meaning. Very often the information does not mean anything to the medium, but they report it as they hear it so the sitter interprets the message. Normally a good medium will not tell the sitter of dire predictions such as someone's pending death. A medium is really acting like a translator between the spirit world and the sitter.

I found the readings were most interesting when I had particular questions as I would receive answers back. I got in the habit of making a list of questions the night before the reading. Once, before I began asking the questions, Pat started by describing where I was the night before when I made up the list. And then she said that Ed wanted me to go to the fourth question first. During those few months, the readings were almost like having conversations with Ed. It was great, but as time went on I realized that although Ed was around me and looking out for me, he was in a different place and his outlook was different from mine in the physical world. I began having fewer and fewer readings. Now I have only one or two readings a year with Pat. I find that this is plenty as I have learned to distinguish when Ed is with me and I have learned to lead life by listening to my intuition which I believe is driven by spirit or God.

Here is a summary of some of the more amazing messages I have received through Pat Gagliardo and a few intuitive friends. They will demonstrate how I have come to believe and recommend that someone seek out a gifted medium to help in healing grief. I have often thought it is odd in our society that people spend thousands of dollars on funerals, but they won't spend any money to talk to their deceased loved ones. I personally have gained a lot of comfort and understanding through the readings.

Since near death experiences and other accounts say that a spirit initially is met by close friends or relatives to help with crossing over, I tried several times to confirm exactly who was there to meet Ed. In the first reading with Pat above, I heard that there were two male spirits, one probably being his Father and the other probably being his Grandfather. But in another reading, I found out there was also a female spirit present whose name was probably Connie. Pat went on to describe Connie as being an extremely fine person with many high quality traits. Pat even said she was God chosen. Ed did have an Aunt Connie who was his mother's sister and who had passed several years before Ed. Since I had only met Aunt Connie once many years ago, I did not really know if this description of her was accurate. I called Ed's sister to see if she would describe Aunt Connie this way. She agreed that this description fit Aunt Connie well.

Shortly after getting this information, I received a call from a good friend, Paula, who had recently been talking to her sister, Angie. I had never met Angie, but I knew that she was very spiritual and had been taking mediumship classes off and on for several years. Paula told me that in a conversation she had been telling Angie about me. She happened to mention that I had been trying to find out who had met Ed when he crossed over. Without knowing anything more, Angie immediately said that Aunt Connie had met him. Somehow that bit of information popped into Angie's head even though she had never heard of Aunt Connie. It had to have somehow come from the spirit world. I have considered this confirmation that Aunt Connie was also there for Ed.

Off and on when Pat has mentioned a particular person, she often gives a description of that person, something unique, either physical or personality traits. Ed's Grandfather, Edgar, was in another reading with the comment that he had been highly revered. I have heard many stories about Edgar in the Hewson family and believe that he truly was a highly revered member of his community.

Another thing I have read is that a person has a premonition of dying before it actually happens, even in the case of sudden deaths. I was curious to know if Ed did. So I asked Pat in one reading. She said that it was between 2 and 3pm when he first had thoughts of dying, but he did not believe it. But he knows now that nothing would have made a difference. When Pat told me this, she knew nothing about how Ed died and she had no idea that Ed had died a little after 7pm. Telling me the timeframe of 2-3pm was completely consistent with the events of that afternoon.

Another time, still being curious as to what Ed experienced, I asked when Ed first knew he was out of his body. Pat said that he realized he was up near the ceiling hovering over his body. This is the most common way people with near death experiences describe it, so this was not earth shaking information. To clarify further, I asked who was in the room at that time. I expected to hear that there were a bunch of men, the paramedics and volunteer firemen who responded to the 911 call. Instead Pat said that there were two. My answer was that was probably later in the hospital when my friend, Beth, was with me. Pat response was "That may be it, but I am not getting a name like Beth. I am hearing a name like Betsy or Sissy. Was Beth ever called by one of those names?" I said I would have to find out.

The next day I asked Beth if she had ever had a nickname like that. When she said no, I assumed that this was inaccurate information. But a week or two later, I suddenly realized that Ed was trying to give Pat the name of "Mugsey," one of my dogs. And the reference to "two" was referring to the two dogs running around the living room while I was calling 911 in the kitchen before the paramedics got there. Beth and I always suspected that Ed had died in the living room before the paramedics got there. I was thrilled to realize that this new information matched.

The middle of March 2004, Pat brought up concern for the health of my older brother, Brien. She said that he was working harder than usual and he is diligent and a perfectionist. These are very accurate adjectives for Brien. Pat went on to say that one of his children, a female who lives away from him, is going to have some good excitement and emotional changes in her life. Brien in fact has just one daughter who is married and lives quite a distance away. I found out the next October that his daughter had just had a baby. That would have been the emotional excitement in March when she was two months pregnant.

Later in March in a reading, Pat asked "Who has a boat?" I told her that I did but I was thinking of selling it. She said that I should make certain to get someone I can trust to help me. Then she went on to say that there is a captain who I can trust who is about six feet tall and has receding white hair. He also has a black onyx ring. I had to stop to think about that description. It was close to one of the captains I had hired the summer before, but I could not remember if he had jewelry. It was not until warmer weather when I first hired Captain Phil again that I was sure he fit the description. That day while we were out in the boat, I got up my nerve and started talking to Phil about my experiences and having readings with a medium. Phil smiled and said he was very familiar with paranormal stuff as in the late 80's he had had a number of friends who were mediums. When I elaborated on the description of him from the reading with Pat, I asked if he had a black onyx ring. He quickly responded, "No, but I'm having one made for me." We were both amazed. A couple of weeks later the next time I saw Phil, he showed me the ring and asked, "Is this the ring you were talking about?"

Phil has become a very good and completely trustworthy friend. We often laugh about the black onyx ring story.

In the same reading, Pat gave me an accurate description of the two timber lots I own in Maine as being in the wilderness and near a lake. But you can't see the lake from these lots. She also knew that I had another piece of property nearby which was a separate piece of land. My lakefront cabin is about a half mile down the road from the timber lots. The warning that followed these descriptions was that I really did not need to sell them, but if I do, then make certain that I get enough for them. She said that there was a neighbor who was interested in them. The next summer a neighbor did express an interest in buying them.

As an animal lover, I have always been concerned as to what happens to our pets when they die. Through my recent experiences and through all these readings, I now believe that the love we have for our pets creates a bond that lasts into the spirit world. There have been a number of readings when Pat has described Ed's big, black and white dog as being with him. Once she tried to interpret the name Ed was saying for the dog, but she said she could not hear the word well and was hearing something like "Rim." Later I realized that the word Ed was saying to her would have been "Grim." Ed often used the nickname, Grim, for Grizz. Pat did not know the dog's name was Grizz and she would never have known the nickname.

Once along with describing Grizz, Pat described my horse, Fleet, as being with Ed. Fleet was the horse who was born on our property and died on our property at age 22. He had been like a dog to us.

Often during a reading with a medium, a name of someone who may or may not have passed will be mentioned. It is often hard to remember immediately who that person might be. After a while I learned the best thing to do is to ask for more detail about how I know the person. An amusing example of this happened in two readings when

I was having one reading a week during that March. In the first of these two, Pat asked if I knew Frank who was on the spirit side. I could not think of who Frank could be and we went onto the next message. The next week, Frank appeared again. This time I asked, "How do I know him?" Pat said that Frank indicated that he was a friend of Ed's when they were young. She went on to describe where Frank had lived in relation to the house where Ed grew up. Since I had not known this person or the neighborhood, I called Ed's sister, Dorothy, that night and gave her the description. She immediately knew who Frank was. With her help, I recognized the name from stories Ed had told me through the years and was glad to have met Frank, even though it was a rather bizarre way.

While having this series of readings, my father's estate was being settled. My father had invested considerable money in bullion gold and silver coins, coins valued mainly for their gold and silver content. When I received my share of the coins, I was contemplating selling a lot of them as the weight of them alone made them hard to store. In one reading, Pat gave me the warning to be careful with the gold coins. She remarked that there was a collection of three coins from the West that I should not sell. I knew right away that this was a reference to some uncirculated Carson City Morgan Silver Dollars which Ed had liked. But since I had received four of them, I wondered why there were only three mentioned. Later for the first time since I received them at the bank, I got these silver dollars out to examine them closer. I found that only three of them were in cases marked "Uncirculated." The fourth was in an unmarked case. I was amazed as the only way Ed could have known only three were uncirculated was to have been with me at the bank.

After some consideration, I decided to sell a lot of the bullion coins and reinvest the money into rare gold coins. About a month after the warning to be careful, in another reading, Pat said she was getting the numbers of 1, 5 and 9 with no explanation. She said it was apparently up to me to know what the numbers referenced. This really perplexed me for a week or so, until I suddenly realized that it was in reference to a rare coin that I was in the process of buying for $15,249. And it made perfect sense that Ed did not want to tell anyone else, including Pat, that I was buying such an expensive coin. So he had given no further explanation.

In all my readings, I have never received any advice on investing money or any numbers to be played in weekly drawings, like Powerball. The only comments on investments were warnings to be careful. In the case of buying the rare coin, I really do not know if Ed was trying to say it was a good investment or a bad one. I just know he knew about it. I have learned from many books that, since the spirit world is based on love and compassion, the focus is not around money and material things. It is considered poor taste to ask for investment advice. No reputable medium will ever ask for or relay such information.

However there are always exceptions. One of Ed's old friends, John, who thought spiritually and who practiced regular meditations, shocked me by letting me know that while he was meditating he had been asking Ed to let him know what stocks to buy. Knowing that I was having a series of readings, John asked if I would ask if Ed had heard him and if Ed would answer his questions. I procrastinated asking such questions but I eventually figured I'd better be able to report back. At first, I asked how the economy would be doing. The answer came back that nothing dramatic would be happening. (Since this reading was on April 15, 2004, we know now that the answer was accurate.) Next I asked, if Ed knew that his friend, John, had been asking Ed questions about stock investments in his meditations. Pat then commented to me that of course I knew that such information really was not important to spirits who have crossed over. But she said Ed knew that John was considering two new stocks. Pat also began laughing and told me that Ed was laughing as he told her that John was always concerned about money. I told Pat that was true. Ed added that it was a good thing that John had been meditating regularly and that I should not tell him anything that would discourage him from meditating. It was totally in Ed's character to have laughed about this.

This was the only time I ever asked any questions on financial matters.

The summer of 2004 I was busy planning the move to my new house and worrying about selling the horse farm. Luckily I was able to work the finances to buy the new house and still own the old place, but I was nervous about how long I would carry the two properties. I was therefore glad whenever I would receive information in readings about how things would be going. In April, I heard that moving should go smoothly. And it did go well in August. In July, I asked when the old house would sell and was told that it would be before the end of the fall. I closed on the old house the middle of November.

I had a reading with Pat the beginning of October when there were some very interested prospective buyers but no signed sales agreement. I asked Pat if these people would buy the farm. Pat commented that these people have had a farm before and there is an elderly person who wants them to buy it. Pat also said that there would be a contingency for the sale of their place but that I should cut them some slack and be lenient in negotiations. She knew that they would have the same depth of feeling and caring for the property that Ed and I had felt. Pat was right about everything. The wife's father lived near my property, loved the property and wanted them to buy it. We did work out a sale based on the contingency of the sale of their current farm in southern Indiana. I cut them some slack and everything worked out perfectly. They are terrific people who love the property.

As I mentioned earlier, there have been times I have received warnings about people and relationships. One time I asked Pat if she could tell me why a particular friend had been acting strangely toward me. Pat said that there was envy toward me and there was tension and ascension in this friend's home life. She warned me not to get caught up and involved in her life. Keeping this warning in mind, I backed off and limited further contact. As time went on, I realized the wisdom of this advice. It saved me from confusion and hurt feelings as the friendship unfortunately fell apart.

Sometimes out of the clear blue, messages have come from friends of friends or some remote relationship. One day in the fall of 2004, Beth called me at work all excited. She had been talking to an old friend whom she had worked with many years ago. Beth said that when she found out this friend was pretty psychic she mentioned my relationship with Ed. Her friend then said, "He was a tall man, wasn't he?" and she said, "He liked to dabble in musical instruments. I am seeing something small, like a keyboard." Ed was 6'4" tall. The word "dabble" is an excellent word to describe Ed with his musical instruments as he played his guitar once in a while and he enjoyed a Casio keyboard. I had given Beth his Casio keyboard since she wanted to take lessons. She loves it. I am sure that Ed was telling her that he was glad she has the keyboard.

As I have mentioned before, my friend, Paula, has a sister, Angie, who has studied becoming a medium. Angie was the one who said that Aunt Connie had met Ed when he crossed over. Another time, Angie told Paula that Ed is an extremely strong communicator. He is with me a lot and wants me to talk and communicate with him. She asked if Ed wore flannel shirts [which he did], if I wear his shirts to bed [I wear his sweatshirts or tee shirts to bed], and if I have dogs. She described to Paula how one dog sleeps next to me with me curled around him, like a half moon. She said that Ed's energy often forms the other half of the moon. Mugsey does sleep on the bed and I usually sleep on my side with Mugsey next to me. How wonderful to think that Ed is there!

After several readings with Pat, she interrupted my questions at the beginning of the reading to say that she could tell that Ed was truly a wonderful man and that she knows he is in a high place. He did what he needed to in this life. She knew that growing up was not easy for him, and as an adult, he could be opinionated but he would help anyone and not necessarily for money. After knowing Ed for 34 years, I know this description is completely accurate. He did have problems growing up. I frequently would get upset with him for continually doing free work for people when he should have been developing his consulting business. And as almost any friend would agree, he could be opinionated.

At the same time, Pat elaborated that, in the almost 25 years she has been doing readings, she could tell Ed and I are two of the closest soulmates she has known. She could count on one hand the number of couples who had this close a relationship. She added that Ed could communicate better than most and she felt that there was a reason why I found her for my readings.

In the beginning of 2007 after I had started this book, I had the chance to go to a small group reading with John Holland, the well known medium. The group had only seven people so we each had a decent amount of time for private readings. When John was in the process of getting messages for me from Ed, he at one point said, "Darn, he is really good at this." I did not say anything, but I sat there thinking, "Yes, I know he has always communicated well both when he was living and many times since his passing."

My feeling is that, through Ed's ability to communicate, it is my destiny to write this book to let people know that relationships live on after physical death.

We are all immortal.

CHAPTER EIGHT

Never Ending Relationship

I don't know why all these things have happened to me to change my thinking from being agnostic. But right now I believe it was my destiny to learn that there is life after death. I can not and will not advocate any particular religion as I am still on my own quest to determine further beliefs, but I do know that our relationships with loved ones live on after physical death. We are all immortal. We merely change form when we die. We just go from the physical to the non-physical. Our bodies are like cars that we get rid of when they become too old or unusable.

I was the chemist who would never believe in any supernatural events. I believe there are several factors which have contributed to my becoming aware of the continuing relationship with Ed. The unusually close bond that Ed and I shared probably drove Ed to want to communicate to let me know he was alive and all right. Of course in the first few months, Ed had to practically hit me over the head with signals to get my attention. Then because throughout his life, Ed was a self taught jack of all trades doing everything from financial consulting to home building to mechanics, I am sure it became a challenge for him to perfect his communications skills. He was known to have been a strong communicator during his physical life and he has continued to be a strong communicator in the afterlife. Someone's basic nature does not change when passing into spirit form. And finally, I have wondered if my unique situation in life of being left alone without any children or close relatives has contributed to the extremely tight, continuing bond with Ed. This may have caused Ed to make sure that I know he is still with me and supporting me.

I have even felt at times that some of Ed's energy has combined with mine as I have felt some of his physical characteristics have appeared in me. This may sound bizarre, but it gives credence to the old saying that two spirits can become one.

But I know that I am not unique with my experiences. I have talked with many people who have had similar happenings. Our loved ones in spirit still love us and are still interested in being part of our lives. I believe strongly they are with us and watching us more than we realize. They may not send signals or make their presence known all the time, but they are often there.

I have had casual conversations with acquaintances who have told me that they know their deceased husbands are still with them even many years after their passing. One of these women told me that she believes her first husband helped her find a second husband and that every so often she still feels his presence. Her first husband passed away more than 20 years ago. Another woman told me that recently while having massage therapy her husband who passed 18 years ago sent the scent of pipe tobacco. Both she and her therapist could smell it.

A continuing relationship like this can and will happen for you, even if you do not notice obvious signs. It is the bond of love between you and your loved one that ties you together, before and after physical death. You were close before, you are still close and you will continue to be close when you pass from the physical.

Don't be afraid to talk to your loved one as you did before. Try asking for signals or things to happen that will confirm his/her presence. It will probably be something unique and meaningful only to you. Sometimes signs are subtle and might be a matter of helping you to make the best decisions. This happens by listening to your "gut" feelings. Follow them and see how things really do work out for the best. Do not second guess your "gut" feelings.

Look for little, unexplainable events and do not be too quick to call them coincidences. When you begin to notice such events, write them down. After a while, you will find your log of events is growing. You will then realize that not all of these events are coincidences.

I believe that many people, who think either that there is no life after death or that their loved one has disappeared into the next life never to return, rob themselves of the comfort of knowing their loved ones are still alive and doing well. These people do not allow themselves to look around and consider the possibility that small, unexplainable events are signals from their loved ones. Since they believe it is not within the realm of reality, they do not notice or acknowledge the events. And to make it worse, they don't dare to discuss these possibilities with friends because they might appear crazy. What a shame! Our loved ones in the spirit world want to continue their relationships with us, but often they are ignored because of preconceived notions. Our relationships do not cease to exist with physical death. But communications are a two way street. You have to be ready to receive them. And in some cases, you have to be ready to forgive and forget in your own mind any issues you had with your loved one.

Remember that your thoughts are powerful. If you are not open to thinking that signals and communications can happen, they either will not happen or you will not believe they happened. Be open to observing and trying things. Send loving thoughts to your loved one along with requests for further communications. Your thoughts will be heard and will be answered.

Initially I was shocked to realize that Ed could read or interpret my thoughts alone. But I have found that I do not need to say things out loud. Many times I have had proof of the power of thoughts. I will be thinking something and get an immediate response from Ed or the spirit world.

Shortly after Steve Irwin, the crocodile hunter, was killed, I saw his wife interviewed on TV. The next day I was working in my garage and was thinking about his wife and how long it would take her to get back to normalcy. At that moment, a cardboard box containing garden utensils fell off the top of a bucket. The box had been sitting on the bucket for months. There was no wind in the garage. I know there was a connection between my thoughts and the box falling. Maybe Ed was telling me that he knew it takes a long time to return to a normal life. I didn't know the exact message, but I felt thankful for getting a response. I always acknowledge and thank Ed for a communication.

Even a few days ago, almost four years after Ed's passing, when I took my car for an oil change, I remembered that there had been several different times when Ed had turned on the car radio either driving into or out of that dealership parking lot. I thought about how neat it would be to have the radio come on by itself to know Ed was there. But it did not happen driving into the lot. By the time the car was ready, I had forgotten all about those thoughts. I started the car and sat with it idling while I recorded the date and mileage of the oil change in a notebook. Then while pulling out of the parking lot, the radio came on. The car had been running for several minutes, so I know I was not mistaking the fact that the radio came on well after the ignition. I know that Ed had been listening to my earlier thoughts and wanted to surprise me when I was not thinking about it. In life, Ed loved to surprise me. Sometimes we would kid each other if something was "too planned."

When spirits cross over, their basic personalities remain the same. For instance, if they had a sense of humor or if they teased in a certain way, they will continue to joke and tease. It is true that their perspectives are different. They know things that we don't. They have gained a universal knowledge which is based on love, compassion and forgiveness. They no longer have feelings like hatred and jealousy. Material things do not mean anything to them now.

However they do want to look out for your welfare while you are here in the physical world. They want to help you live well while growing spiritually and to help you become a better person. Listen to the little voice inside you or that "gut" feeling when you are making decisions. Spirits close to you are trying to steer your life in this way. You may often find that ignoring your "gut" feeling creates situations full of hardships and negative results. I find when I am making a big decision I know it is the correct decision when I have a calm, peaceful feeling about it.

Deceased loved ones do not want to see you grieve for extended periods of time or have you become bitter with living life without them. They want you to go on with your life and enjoy it. They will not be jealous or upset if you establish new relationships and have new joys in life. You are a unique individual with your own strengths. You need to proceed. I know this is hard, but your loved one is there to help you.

If you decide as I did to establish further communications by hiring a medium, make sure that you find someone who is reputable. And keep in mind that there is a big difference in the abilities of mediums. Some have been chosen or blessed with far greater communication skills. Judge for yourself if the messages you receive are accurate and sound typical for your loved ones. Be ready to try different mediums to find one that feels right. Remember that phone readings can be just as accurate as readings in person. So don't be afraid to try them.

And I have a few more words about readings with mediums. Many books by mediums say that it is a good idea to wait at least six months after a person passes to get messages from that person/spirit. Sooner than that, the spirit who has recently passed may not be oriented enough to communicate well through a medium. Effective communications are supposed to take extra energy and effort for the spirit. When you have a reading, the medium is casting out a request to communicate to the spirit world for spirits who are connected with you. The medium cannot control which spirits "show up" or which ones communicate first. The loved one you want to hear from may not communicate. If that is the case, don't be discouraged. Try additional readings, but remember to judge the accuracy for yourself.

When I was having a lot of readings, I received a number of messages to get in touch with an old friend or a relative as they were likely having some health issues. This kind of information is always disturbing, but I believe it should not be given to the person himself. Several times, I did contact the friend or relative who I had not talked to for a while and found out that they were perfectly fine. After thinking about receiving such information, my belief is that, since the spirit world does not know about time, the health issues may still happen but not for a long time, maybe a few years. So when or if you receive information about someone's health, keep it in the back of your mind and do not communicate doomsday thoughts. If you are really concerned, keep that person in your prayers.

Don't forget that you can and should ask questions during a reading, particularly if you need clarification for a message you just received. The communication through the medium can be two way, but be careful not to ask questions that would reveal too much information to the medium. A reputable medium likes to be sure to have received accurate messages from the spirit world and not from assumptions they have made from your comments. At the same time, mediums need confirmation from you that what they believe they are hearing makes sense to you. Another thing I found is that it is best not to ask questions that have "Yes" or "No" answers. When I did, I realized that either I did not trust the "Yes/No" answer I received or I tended to get ambiguous answers instead of "Yes" or "No".

Also keep in mind that you have free will and a responsibility to live your life to the best of your ability. Your loved ones in the spirit world will not directly tell you how to lead your life. A good example of this happened when I was frustrated and stressed out about my job. I asked Ed in a reading with Pat what I should do about work, and I received the answer that I have to trust my feelings. A couple of weeks later when I dreamed about our dog, Grizz, getting into a swimming pool, the message from the dream was that I needed to trust myself the way Grizz had trusted me. I was not told to retire early, but once I made that decision, I felt at peace with it. I know I had the responsibility to trust myself and to make the decision. Do not expect a medium to tell you how to live. You might get warnings through the medium, but it is up to you to decide how to proceed.

If you are in the process of grieving the loss of a loved one, I know it is not easy and it takes a long time. At times, I still find myself wishing Ed were here in the physical world enjoying retirement as we had planned. But then, I have to catch myself and remember that he *is* here with me much of the time. I know he is not with me all the time as he has new things to do in his spirit life, but he is with me when I need him and when he wants to experience life and adventures with me. He is also with me when I need help making decisions in life. I now realize that I am a separate immortal soul with the responsibility to grow through my own victories and defeats in this physical life. When the time is right, I will join Ed and others in the spirit life. But in the meantime, I am continuing my spiritual journey into further understanding so I can offer the world a better person while I am here.

I hope that reading of my experiences will make you open to a new understanding that spirit signals and communications will happen for you as well. You will be comforted in discovering for yourself that you truly have a never ending relationship with your loved one.

Remember, we are all IMMORTAL.

Afterword

Life has many twists and turns, many of which are hard to accept and understand at the time, but in the long run, it is possible to see how it was meant to be. I believe that it was my destiny to lose my husband, Ed, and to be left alone to learn how to live more independently. I was alone facing the loss of my husband and best buddy. The recovery took a long time, but with the help of Ed in spirit, I did it. My outlook on life has changed tremendously in the years since his death. I would like to think that through writing this book, I can help others through their grief to see and feel the healing of the spirit world.

I have grown and moved on, but I still miss Ed and look forward to his periodic signals to say he is around. I don't have the need for readings from a medium any more and I feel I have read enough spiritually related books. I have my own beliefs which hopefully will help to guide me through the ups and downs of the rest of my life.

Off and on in the medium readings I had in the first few years after Ed's death, I was told that when the time was right Ed would find me a companion. After about 4 years, I began to think it would be nice to meet someone to go out to dinner or other places with. Having just learned about affirmations through Louise Hay's video, *You Can Heal Your Life*, I created my affirmation of the type of man I would like to meet. The next spring, I met a widower, Donald, who had cabin a mile from my Maine cabin. Being both retired, we saw each other constantly that summer and got married in October. Donald is exactly same as the man I described in my affirmations. We are true soulmates. We cannot believe how lucky we are to have each found a second soulmate in life. Donald's wife had passed away in 2002 from cancer. Donald is not the same as Ed and I am not the same as Donald's late wife. But our temperaments and personalities are almost exactly the same. We are not sure that our relationship would have worked when we were younger, but right now we are perfect for each other. I think this was my destiny.

I hope that I can help others work through their grieving for their lost loved one. Life can and will get better.

About the Author

Diana Hewson is relaxing and enjoying life after retiring from many years in the high tech industry in middle management. She now lives with her second husband and second soulmate with their dogs in the seacoast area of New Hampshire. They both love spending lots of time every summer at their waterfront cabin in the wilderness of Maine, as well as travelling and visiting remote areas of the world, such as Antarctica. Diana feels that all her research into life after death and the spiritual world after her first husband's death has allowed her to understand herself spiritually and to learn to accept life's ups and downs. She is hoping that this book will help others work through the grief from losing a loved one by understanding there is life after death and we are all truly immortal.

BIBLIOGRAPHY

Altea, Rosemary, *Proud Spirit*, New York, NY: Eagle Brook, an imprint of William Morrow and Company Inc., 1997

Gagliardo, Patricia, *Pebbles on the Path*, Lincoln, NE: Writers Press Club, an imprint of iUniverse.com, Inc., 2000

Guggenheim, Bill & Judy, *Hello From Heaven*, New York, NY: Bantam Books, 1995

Hickman, Martha Whitmore, *Healing After Loss*, New York, NY: Perennial, an imprint of HarperCollins Publishers, 2002

Holland, John, *born KNOWING*, Carlsbad, CA: Hay House, Inc., 2003

Kubler-Ross, Elizabeth, *On Death and Dying*, New York, NY: Scribner, 1969

Moody, Raymond A., Jr., M.D., *Life After Life*, New York, NY: HarperCollins Publishers, 2001

Morse, Melvin, M.D., *Closer To The Light*, New York, NY: Ivy Books, 1990

Newton, Michael, *Journey of Souls*, St Paul, MN: Llewellyn Publications, 1996

Tolle, Eckhart, *The Power of NOW*, Novato, CA: New World Library, 2004

Van Praagh, James, *Healing Grief*, New York, NY: New American Library, 2001

Van Praagh, James, *Talking to Heaven*, New York, NY: Signet, 1999

Watkins, Susan M., *Conversations with Seth*, Needham, MA: Moment Point Press, Inc., 2005

Weiss, Brian L., M.D., *Many Lives, Many Masters*, New York, NY: Fireside, 1988